Language and communication are at the heart of the human experience. The United States must educate students who are linguistically and culturally equipped to communicate successfully in a pluralistic American society and abroad. This imperative envisions a future in which ALL students will develop and maintain proficiency in English and at least one other language, modern or classical. Children who come to school from non-English backgrounds should also have opportunities to develop further proficiencies in their first language.

STATEMENT OF PHILOSOPHY,
**AMERICAN COUNCIL ON THE
TEACHING OF FOREIGN LANGUAGES**

Published by Seidlitz Education
P.O. Box 166827
Irving, TX 75016
www.seidlitzeducation.com

For related titles and support materials visit www.seidlitzeducation.com.

4.21

(7) STEPS to a
LANGUAGE-RICH, INTERACTIVE
Foreign Language
Classroom

Strategies for Teachers of
LANGUAGES OTHER THAN ENGLISH (LOTE)

BY ANNA MATIS WITH JOHN SEIDLITZ

CONTRIBUTIONS BY ELIZABETH JOHNSON

*To my French language teachers who
paved the way for my journey:*
Mme Jean Ann Johnson (Creekwood MS),
Mme Muriel MacKay (Kingwood 9th),
Mme Patricia Corres (Kingwood HS),
Dr. Suzanne Chamier (Southwestern University)

*To my foreign language teacher mentors who
so graciously imparted their knowledge to me:*
Mme Frances Novier Baldwin, Mme Amy Smith,
Mme Morgan Marthaler Steele, and Sra. Gloria Tran

*To my foreign language methodology
professors, for teaching me how language
truly develops:*
Dr. Veronica Sardegna, Dr. Elaine Horwitz,
Dr. Diane Pulido, and Dr. Dianne Schallert

ACKNOWLEDGMENTS

John, thank you for making all of this possible. Your passion and enthusiasm serve as the heart of this endeavor. Thank you for inviting me to be a part of this amazing team of not only colleagues, but individuals who have become dear friends and family. Meg, for your love of language learning, ruthless editing skills, and strict adherence to the Oxford comma. John and I are better for it. Anne-Charlotte, for being a mind reader and quite literally pulling images and designs out of my head to appear in print before my very eyes.

Bill Perryman, thank you for bringing these engaging activities to life. And Yvonne Jaubert Smith, my dear friend and social studies teacher extraordinaire, for introducing me to Bill so I could see his magic for myself. Elizabeth Johnson, for gifting us with your experience in theory, practice, and writing. You made this book stronger. And to KC O'Brien, for introducing Elizabeth to us!

To the educators in the field who work tirelessly so our language learners can benefit from these strategies that open the door for success, thank you for all that you do. To the school districts that continue to support our work, we are so grateful for your energy around this project. We are especially grateful for LOTE directors Kim Lybarger (Lamar CISD), Allison Ginn (Frisco ISD), and Bibiana Bermudez (Boerne ISD) for being our first cheerleaders.

To my parents, Steve and Eva, thank you for your endless love and support in everything that I set my mind to. My brother, Steve, for inspiring me to be a better writer. You are more talented than you know. Lastly, to Dr. Craig Mullenix, for offering me the opportunity to transform my life as an educator, and introducing me to the students in my classroom who inspired me to delve into this research and become a stronger language teacher. Thank you for having faith in me.

— Anna

table *of* contents

To learn a language is to have one more window from which to look at the world.

— CHINESE PROVERB

The ability to communicate with respect and cultural understanding in more than one language is vital to successful interactions among diverse groups of people locally, nationally, and internationally. Foreign language learning is thus a desirable skill not only to give speakers a competitive edge in their careers but also to enable successful cross-cultural communication among people around the world. Yet, although this view is widely shared, many people still hesitate to learn a foreign language because it is often perceived as an insurmountable goal and/or a tedious task. 7 *Steps to a Language-Rich, Interactive Foreign Language Classroom* facilitates the learning process with easy-to-remember-and-use, research-based strategies. As a multilingual speaker, teacher, trainer, and author, Anna Matis has in-depth, experiential knowledge of what it takes to learn a foreign language. Full of practical examples and activities, this book is certainly a valuable resource for foreign language learners and teachers around the world.

For more than 25 years, I have taught graduate-level teacher education courses and courses in English as a second and foreign language to learners of all ages and proficiency levels in the U.S and Argentina. Additionally, I have held several graduate-level positions, including teaching assistant at the University of Illinois at Urbana-Champaign, lecturer and assistant professor at the University of Texas at Austin (2009-2014), and visiting assistant professor at the University of Pittsburgh (2014-present). In the last decade, my research has focused on exploring the effects of individual learner differences, teaching methodologies, and instructional technology tools that support autonomous second and foreign language learning and teaching. I have published my research in prestigious, peer-reviewed journals and methodology books and discussed my findings at many national and international scholarly gatherings and workshops. During my career I have had the pleasure of reading, studying, and teaching many books on foreign language learning methodology. I have to confess that Anna's book has quickly become one of my favorites.

I met Anna in 2012. She was taking my course on teaching foreign languages at the University of Texas at Austin. I remember Anna's contributions to the course quite vividly. She was not only an avid and successful learner but also an enthusiastic participant during class discussions and group activities, especially when it came to critiquing and reviewing different language learning methodologies. It came as no surprise to me that she was one of the first to volunteer for ESL tutoring lessons as part of a research study I was conducting at the time. This volunteer experience, alongside the practice lessons she gave during class, allowed me to closely study her teaching skills and effectiveness. Her work was exemplary. Anna exhibited superb skills in activity and lesson design implementation. I knew then that she had an excellent career ahead of her. Since Anna graduated with an M.A. in foreign language education, I have followed her career with great enthusiasm. Before she became an author and trainer as well as product development manager for Seidlitz Education, she worked as an ESL instructional coach, a bilingual/ESL specialist, and a program manager for an education service center in Austin, Texas. Since 2013, she has presented many times locally and nationally on best practices for quality language instruction. This book is the product of her vast academic and professional experiences in the field of second and foreign language education.

When Anna asked me to provide a foreword for her book, I jumped at the opportunity to express my sincere admiration for her work and her outstanding career in professional development. *7 Steps to a Language-Rich, Interactive Foreign Language Classroom* is a book written by a teacher for teachers. Anna's clear and informal writing style makes learning entertaining and memorable, and her curious and reflective mind permeates the book from beginning to end. The book's useful organization and colorful layout make it easy to find all the relevant information, and each of its seven easy-to-follow steps is followed by pressing questions and answers informed by research, reflection, and practice. Without a doubt, teachers will find it easy to incorporate the many creative ideas, resources, and activities showcased in the book into their foreign language learning curriculum.

7 Steps to a Language-Rich, Interactive Foreign Language Classroom is a must-have tool for foreign language teacher trainers as well as pre-service and in-service foreign language teachers looking for research-based strategies, effective and creative resources, and a foundational understanding of second language learning theories. This book is indeed a much needed and welcome addition to our field.

Veronica G. Sardegna
Visiting Assistant Professor
of Foreign Language Education
University of Pittsburgh

While attending high school in Misawa, Japan, I started learning Spanish from Señora Snyder. I credit her with introducing me to Spanish language and culture. My love of languages, however, began as a child when my dad first taught me some Greek (my grandmother was from Athens). Soon after, while my dad was stationed in Sembach, Germany, I acquired a little German. Spanish class in high school with Señora Snyder was simply the next step, and although I wasn't living in a Spanish-speaking country, I was able to acquire enough Spanish to be able to communicate with native speakers. I eventually become fluent in Spanish when I moved to south Texas where I went to college, learned Arabic, and minored in Middle Eastern Studies. I think my experience is an example of the importance of foreign language teachers as multiple cultures increasingly interact with each other across the globe.

Foreign language teachers have the unique opportunity to be bridge builders between cultures. This is why I am so honored to introduce this book. It fulfills a dream of mine: helping to improve foreign language education. The book, *7 Steps to a Language-Rich, Interactive Foreign Language Classroom*, provides a framework to help teachers build these bridges. Written by Anna Matis, an educator with extensive experience as both a foreign language teacher and bilingual/ESL education specialist, this book is meant to help teachers build their students' motivation and ability to communicate in the foreign language classroom.

The book is built on the core concepts presented in a book I co-authored with Bill Perryman: *7 Steps to a Language-Rich, Interactive Classroom*. That book outlines a framework for encouraging students to listen, speak, read, and write using academic language in content-area classrooms. It was primarily focused on supporting teachers of English language learners and economically disadvantaged students. However, when Anna approached me about adapting the original 7 Steps, I thought, "Wow! What an idea." Anna's work in this book would connect my experience with language acquisition with her expertise as a teacher of a foreign language class. I knew this approach would be as effective for foreign language teachers as it had been for ESL teachers.

Anna's *7 Steps to a Language-Rich, Interactive Foreign Language Classroom* is a book that provides LOTE (Languages Other Than English) teachers with a specific set of concrete strategies they can use to enable students to interact with confidence in a new language, complete with research supporting each of the seven steps. Each strategy is simple yet powerful. When foreign language teachers start to use the steps, they are going to be surprised by how much these simple, small changes can make a difference. Teachers who are just beginning to teach a foreign language will benefit from the specificity of the strategies and techniques described in the book. Teachers with more experience will also find some new ideas and ways to refine existing classroom practices.

I was thrilled to have been asked to contribute to this book, as I truly believe it will make a difference for teachers and students in foreign language classes.

Paris, France

A LITTLE HISTORY
by Anna

I picked up my first French-language dictionary at a book fair in the seventh grade.

Most of my middle school peers at the time were beginning to take Spanish as their foreign language elective, but I knew I wanted to try something different. Growing up in a Hungarian immigrant family, hearing languages other than English was not foreign to me at all; in fact, it was more of a comfort. My relationship with the French language, however, went a little deeper. In my youth, I remember hearing French spoken as the official language of both summer and winter Olympic games, as well as World Cup tournaments every four years.

Shortly after relocating to Houston upon emigrating to the United States, we befriended a friendly family of French origin, the Noviers. Their language and cuisine quickly became an integral part of my childhood. My experience with French culture also grew with exposure to French Impressionism paintings at the Museum of Fine Arts in Houston. I wanted to visit Paris, the iconic capital of France.

My first French classroom experience was exactly how you would imagine such a setting to be. Madame Jean Ann Johnson created an environment where French music played upon entry through her doors, and pictures of Paris were interspersed together with historical posters of the world. We were greeted with her delightful French accent, a complete surprise to students like myself, who had first known her as our sixth grade social studies teacher. We were invited to select a French name that we would be called for the remainder of the semester. I selected Sylvie. The name stuck with me for years. By tenth grade, in French II Honors, I would switch to Giselle, as I loved how it "sounded" very French.

Little did I know at the time, but the selection of French names for each student on the first day of class actually served two purposes. First, it was a highly engaging introduction to the sounds of the French language, giving students an immediate opportunity to practice and perfect their French pronunciation. Second, it was a low-stress opportunity to not only receive comprehensible input in the target language, but it also provided an opportunity to practice comprehensible output (more on this on pg. 25).

Then in high school, I met Madame Patricia Corres. She changed my life. She is the epitome of the perfect foreign language teacher. Mme. Corres embodied a European flair, and interestingly enough, she also spoke perfectly fluent Spanish (partly due to her husband, Lucilo, a witty Spaniard). She would often wear the perfect neck scarf to compliment her outfit (a staple of French fashion, bien sûr) and spoke to us in a tone that was both serious and demure, with an air of kindness. For the remainder of my time in high school, Mme. Corres would be my entry point to French art,

music, cinema, customs...and conjugations. In an extraordinary bit of serendipity, my worlds collided when the Novier, Corres, and Matis families all befriended one another. Frances Novier, our first and dearest family friend from back when we had just moved to Houston, became the French teacher at a neighboring high school. My life would never be the same. Dinner parties, Fourth of July BBQ's, and family gatherings would now consist of Mesdames Novier and Corres speaking at the table in French, discussing students, lesson plans, and the general state of affairs of foreign language teaching in suburban Houston, Texas.

I got into teaching through a circuitous route, and it was a few short years before I, too, could join in on the dinner conversation. I was the new French teacher at MacArthur Ninth Grade School, a first for this campus, and Mme's Novier and Corres shared with me their lesson plans, CDs, books, and maps, along with posters of Paris and the rest of France. I displayed these items proudly as I set up my new classroom (see photos on pgs. 15-18), and I felt it was coming full circle. I would share this passion for the language with my upcoming French learners, and they would be well on their way to being French speakers!

Photo courtesy of Anna Matis.

Or so I thought...

Continuez! —→

Photo courtesy of Anna Matis

FACTORS THAT AFFECT

Paris, France

Second Language Acquisition

I crafted a small faux living room in the back corner, complete with a bistro table, curtains, and a tall, slender lamp all labeled in perfect French environmental print. French Impressionism art prints lined the wall. Replicas of the Eiffel Tower, along with a photograph of me standing in front of the iconic beauty on my first trip to Paris, adorned the shelves.

In setting up my own classroom, I carried with me vivid memories of my own first French classes: waiting in anticipation to select my French name for the year, and receiving my syllabus with all the topics and material that were to be covered. French class had been my respite from the more dry and dreaded classes in a typical high school day. I was ready for my students.

Unfortunately, once they arrived, the first days didn't go exactly as I expected. French class didn't seem to mean as much to my students as it had meant to me. Many of my students were very reluctant to speak the language, and they were even more unwilling to write. Vocabulary was regurgitated but then quickly forgotten. We moved through the routine of unit-by-unit learning seen in many foreign language classrooms, such as learning about food and culture, and — of course — buying tickets at the train station for a journey they would never take. But actual French language development? Forget it.

What was I doing wrong?

As a high school French teacher, motivating students was tricky - not because I wasn't funny or engaging (which I was) or lacking determination for my students to succeed (which I didn't); there was something else happening. I was unaware that requiring a greater understanding of my students'

Photo courtesy of Anna Matis.

backgrounds and ambitions would prove to be paramount to both my teaching and their learning.

If pictured as a bell curve, the majority of my French I student population was composed of students with what I'd call a hybrid-linguistic-proficiency in their first languages. One end of the curve consisted of students who often switched languages between English and Spanish while learning French. Many of these students were enrolled in the course because of scheduling conflicts as opposed to genuine interest. The opposite end of the curve consisted of gifted and talented students (many of whom were also bilingual) who were bursting with motivation for language learning.

I wondered why the kids weren't motivated to learn French the same way I was. The majority of my students came from low-income

backgrounds. Perhaps that was a factor? Many students came into my classroom without a command of academic English or Spanish. Others had personal issues they were facing outside the classroom walls. I came to find out that while many of these things were true, they were also beyond my control. As a teacher, I was concerned about all factors that could affect second language acquisition (SLA). I spent a lot of time thinking and worrying about my students' age, native language proficiency, demographics, socioeconomic status (SES), literacy level, and other related factors. But could I change these things? I didn't realize at the time, although looking back now it's obvious, that these are factors I just didn't have control over.

> *What I could control, however, was what is called M.A.Q.*

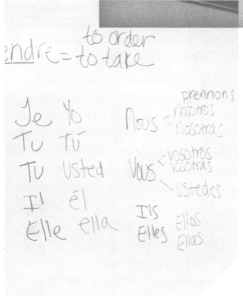

Photos courtesy of Anna Matis.

What is M.A.Q.?

**M.A.Q. stands for
Motivation,
Access to Language, and
Quality of Instruction.**
Understanding the power of M.A.Q. was the first key to transforming the way I viewed and experienced second language instruction. M.A.Q. is also the foundation to effectively implementing the *7 Steps to a Language-Rich, Interactive Foreign Language Classroom.* Once I made this connection, I could then use this information to more effectively scaffold my instruction and create access points to the target language for my various groups of learners.

So how did I discover these 7 Steps, and why are they so pivotal to language instruction?

After completing my graduate work in foreign language education, specializing in heritage language learning and teaching English as a second language, I attended a workshop that changed everything for me. As a new instructional coach charged with guiding teachers on adapting their content and instruction to meet the needs of language learners, I needed more tools in my toolbelt.

My first day on the job was district staff development day, and I walked in to grab a front table seat for the *7 Steps to Language-Rich, Interactive Classroom* training led by John Seidlitz.

Within the first 20 minutes, I knew I had walked into a gold mine. By lunchtime, I knew I'd found my holy grail. By the end of the day,

John had a room of 120 teach[ers] turning and talking, taking p[art in] conversations with academic [...] reading, writing, and speaking about the solar system in Italian. I was so intrigued that I signed up for his next workshop two weeks later for ESL teachers. After another language-immersion simulation, we were reading, writing, and speaking in German. How was this possible?

It was the magic of the 7 Steps! The integral function of the 7 Steps is to build a communicative classroom environment where students are not only motivated to participate but have access points to use the target language (English, French, Spanish, German, etc.) in a way that is comprehensible to them and scaffolded for their various language levels. Visuals and vocabulary are tools for building comprehension, and easy-to-implement structures are in place for moving through the modes of communication. **The 7 Steps aren't so much a methodology but norms that increase the comprehensible input that students are receiving while providing low-stress opportunities for output.**

After attending these trainings, the 7 Steps became the cornerstone on which I would coach my content-area, foreign language, and ESL teachers and later build my professional development sessions as a Bilingual/ESL specialist.

Again, the 7 Steps are not a methodology. They are a framework for you to work in that will allow you to access some of the best theoretical knowledge in second language acquisition with practical applicability to the foreign language classroom. They are learning and teaching strategies for all modes of communication and for all levels of language acquisition. The 7 Steps and their explanations in this book draw from SLA research and are structured around M.A.Q.

In writing this book, my goal is to share with foreign language teachers (both novice and seasoned) this framework that can transform your classroom into an interactive and communicative environment in which students are engaging in functional language and academic structures in the target language from day one. Within this framework, systems are inherently in place to randomize and rotate so that all students, even the reluctant ones, have supports at their level to effortlessly engage in the language learning. Implementation of this framework can help your students access and engage in language acquisition and thereby grow from novice to intermediate to advanced language users. Essentially, I'm writing the book I wish I could have had as a LOTE teacher, and I hope to share the language-learning benefits of these steps with those in the field today.

Allez! ⟶

Motivation

When it comes to foreign languages, motivation is the primary impetus to initiate student learning, and it is also the driving force to continue that learning (Dörnyei & Csizér, 1998). It is also one of the most important factors associated with language-learning achievement. For this context, motivation refers to the objectives, reasons, or impulses that drive an individual to achieve (Gardner & Tremblay, 1994).

Interestingly, research has found that the degree of motivation seems to be more important than type of motivation (i.e., instrumental or integrative). If students are learning the foreign language to add this knowledge to a résumé in hopes of increasing future career opportunities, then per the seminal research of Gardner and Lambert (1972), this desire to learn is based primarily on instrumental motivation, as students have a pragmatic reason for learning the language and performing better in a job. Simply wanting to obtain the required foreign language course requirement is also a form of instrumental motivation. Integrative motivation refers to students' desire to integrate into the target culture and get to know the people who speak the language. Students who wish to study abroad in a foreign country may want to learn the target language in order to better assimilate once there.

An additional factor to consider is the distinction between *intrinsic* and *extrinsic* motivation. Students with intrinsic motivation are motivated to engage and remain engaged in an activity purely for enjoyment, while students with extrinsic motivation engage in an activity because of external circumstances, such as receiving a reward. Researchers also cite the desire to improve pronunciation skills as a significant motivator across all factors (Sardegna, Lee, & Kusey, 2014).

Gardner's more current research (2010) also divides motivation into three components: effort, drive, and affect. Effort refers to "time on task," while drive is the learner's desire to achieve language proficiency. Affect is the emotional connection to the language and language study. Affect is, perhaps, the most critical, because it determines the student's willingness to engage in the process (drive) and the amount of time she/he is willing to dedicate to language study (effort). It is the emotional factor that accelerates or impedes the process of language learning.

Anna in Paris, 2004.

MOTIVATION AND COMMUNICATION IN THE FOREIGN LANGUAGE CLASSROOM

In middle school, the highlight of my day was walking out of my U.S. history class and into French 1A with Madame Johnson. Don't get me wrong, as thrilling as it was to hear about the Articles of Confederation from Coach Ray sitting behind his desk, entering French class was an escape for me. In the French classroom, surrounded by posters of the Eiffel Tower and soft French music, and participating in French dialogues, I felt as if I were immersed in French culture. My desire to experience this culture in person ignited my motivation to learn to communicate in the language to the best of my ability.

Many years later, as a classroom teacher, this colorful environment and immediate introduction to the culture were tools that I used as motivators for my students. From an early introduction to French customs and attitudes, foods, sights, and of course the infamous French accent, some of my beginning learners were quickly hooked. They desired to know more about the target culture and language, with hopes of seeing and using it for themselves one day.

I conducted a goal-setting activity at the end of the first week, where students had to write about why they wanted to learn French. The majority of the respondents expressed a desire to go to France and speak with a French person — preferably without making a lot of mistakes. This motivator is well summarized in Gardner's model component of integrative motivation, which shows a "positive disposition" toward the L2 (second language) group along with the desire to not only interact with but also become similar to members of that community (Dörnyei & Czisér, 1998). Fostering a classroom environment in which students could feel that this would be an attainable goal was something that I did to not only remove students' hesitations toward learning and speaking the language but, more importantly, to instill a passion to embrace the language and culture. **High student motivation was enhanced by factors I had control over, like providing a welcoming, communicative classroom environment and maintaining a high quality of instruction.** The success my students felt when they were able to communicate led to increased motivation. There was no reason for me to be discouraged if my students initially arrived with low levels of motivation.

> With regard to students beginning their L2 language study at a later age (as is the case in a majority of K–12 schooling environments in the United States), studies have shown that achieving near-native levels has been related to "unusually high motivation and high quality of instruction" (Ortega, 2009).

MOTIVATION AND READING IN THE FOREIGN LANGUAGE CLASSROOM

Something I hadn't yet considered was whether or not I was fostering future readers in my class. Was I promoting any kind of positive experience with reading in the target language? Research by Bamford and Day (2004) has found that that students who read in a second language achieve several advantages:

> Develop into more confident readers

> Write better

> Improve upon their listening and speaking abilities

> Acquire richer vocabulary

> Develop positive attitudes toward the target language

> Increase motivation to study the new language

Motivation is thus a key factor to consider when fostering reading development in L2 learners (Grabe, 2004; Pulido, 2009). The research of Guthrie and Wigfield suggests that avid readers may strive for higher grades and recognition, which would foster both intrinsic and extrinsic motivation (Grabe, 2009). Also, those learners with high intrinsic motivation have higher comprehension and are more engaged with texts (Meece & Holt, 1993). **They also read more.**

My studies in the connection between motivation and L2 reading showed that my students who loved to read saw greater success in this area. If they were products of schooling environments that implemented extensive reading programs into the curriculum in younger grades, the students developed a love of reading early on. Then this enthusiasm could transfer when they began learning to read in a second language.

The educational context in which a student is raised affects reading development because of print exposure. Students from lower SES backgrounds may not have received adequate exposure to texts in the primary language, which research has shown to affect literacy development (Adams, 1994). Students learning their primary languages are exposed to millions of words per year in classrooms, books, cartoons, etc. (Grabe, 2009). L2 students learning to read are not exposed to a fraction of this amount unless they are completely immersed in the L2 environment. The greater number of words in print that a learner can be exposed to in the school and home environment, the greater word recognition and vocabulary development can progress in the L2. Thus sociocultural context greatly affects the development of reading in both languages.

As teachers, we can do our best to create a classroom environment where students want to read and learn. We can provide near-constant exposure to books, cartoons, advertisements, etc. in the target language. This exposure to authentic texts will extend to our students' L2 reading development. Additional communication skills will be improved with vocabulary recognition, and functional language in the form of chunks will also be introduced. This will add to the immersive nature of our foreign language classrooms.

Tapping into intrinsic motivation is key for a student to be successful in not only L2 reading but in all language domains. A classroom context that is pleasant and supportive, and that builds interest that increases student motivation, is crucial (Dörnyei, 2001, as cited by Grabe, 2009). The 7 Steps will help you build this classroom context.

Barcelona, Spain

oto courtesy of Anna Matis.

Access to Language

As other LOTE teachers can surely relate, I loved teaching my students about the target language, from its history and origin — complete with quirks and eccentricities — to its presence in art, cinema, and popular culture. Students learned the perfect scripted dialogue to use at a moment's notice when ordering in a cafe or when searching for the Metro.

But what happened when the skit ended and we moved on to the next unit or chapter? Very little retention of target structures and grammar rules. When students not enrolled in my class would ask my French learners to "speak French," they could recite vocabulary from last week's dialogue, but they could not carry on fluid, communicative conversations outside of memorized scripts. As it turns out, my students were learning about the language but not actually acquiring the language.

Dr. Michelle Yzquierdo (2017, p. 78) expands further on this intricate balance of learning versus acquisition:

"Did you take a foreign language in high school or college? Are you currently fluent in that language? For most of us, the answer is no. Why is that? How did most of us spend two or more years 'learning' a language that we now, for the most part, cannot speak or understand? Part of the answer can be explained by Krashen's theory of second language acquisition (1981). Essential to Krashen's theory is the difference between learning a language and acquiring a language...Language learning is the product of formal and systematic instruction in vocabulary and grammar. Language acquisition, even for a second language, is a subconscious process very similar to the process children undergo when they acquire their first language. Acquisition requires meaningful, authentic interaction in the target language, while learning is a conscious process resulting in knowledge of the language. One might learn such things as grammar, syntax, and form, for example. Learning the language is what we experienced in most of our formal language courses in high school and college, and acquisition is what begins to happen when you start 'picking up' Spanish on your vacation to Mexico."

This distinction between language learning and acquisition was what I failed to understand. My students needed access to the language so they could not only learn but also utilize and acquire target structures, phrases, and vocabulary words. Both processes are important in a foreign language classroom. Students benefit from understanding about a language, but especially from the opportunities to acquire fluency through listening, reading, writing, and speaking. When we provide students with access to language, it simply means that we are equipping them with entry points of comprehension in a target language and approachable language "tools" for response and language creation. Simply put, it is comprehensible input with low-stress opportunities for output.

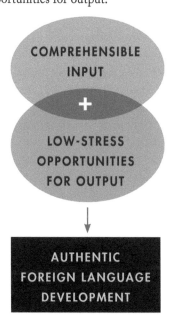

COMPREHENSIBLE INPUT

Comprehensible input is one of the most critical concepts of second language acquisition to understand when teaching a new language. The term refers to any written or spoken messages that students understand in a foreign language because of the context. It is part of the language acquisition hypothesis first proposed by Stephen Krashen (1982). His theory of second language acquisition is comprised of five models: the acquisition-learning distinction (mentioned above), the monitor hypothesis, the natural order hypothesis, the input hypothesis, and the affective filter hypothesis. In this book, the two most significant models are the last two.

The input hypothesis suggests that we acquire more language only when we are exposed to comprehensible input. Krashen believed that input was best received when it was slightly challenging for the language learner. This is referred to as "i+1" which means "input plus one." Spoken or written messages in the target language should be slightly above the level of the student. If the input is not challenging at all, no language development occurs. If it is too challenging, the language learner won't understand the message. This language, which is just slightly beyond a student's current level of competency, becomes comprehensible when meaning is attained with the help of visual cues, gestures, understandable rates of speech, and realia, just to name a few (Hadley, 2001). When the teacher implements learning strategies that effectively bridge the language gap for the students, lessons become more comprehensible.

Learners hear and see language in a communicative context that they process for meaning. We call this type of language input. Input cannot be equated with the staple of much traditional language teaching: explanation about grammar, presentation of vocabulary lists, practice, fill in the blanks, and so on. For mental representation to develop, learners have to hear and see language as it is used to express meaning. There are no shortcuts; representation cannot be taught in the traditional sense of teaching. Input does not guarantee acquisition, however. Nothing does. But acquisition cannot happen in the absence of input

(VanPatten, 2014).

THE AFFECTIVE FILTER

Additionally, in order to effectively provide comprehensible input in a foreign language classroom, it is essential to understand the role of the affective filter in second language learning and acquisition. The affective filter has been described as "an imaginary barrier" between a language learner and new input. The barrier consists of negative motivational and emotional factors that interfere with a person's ability to receive comprehensible input. For example, if a person is feeling embarrassed and stressed about having to speak aloud in front of peers, it would be hard for that person to receive comprehensible input. To receive input, the language learner needs to be relaxed and concentrating more on meaning and less on form for the time being. "Flow" theory describes that optimal, psychological state in which individuals are fully immersed and enjoying an activity (Csíkszentmihályi, 2009).The more language learners are in

a state of "flow" and are concentrating on meaning, the more input they receive. The more stressed they are, the less input they receive. This is why it is important for LOTE teachers to ensure that they are taking the right steps to lower their students' affective filters.

In more instances than not, the foreign language classroom (especially at the secondary level) can be a source of anxiety for students. Speaking out loud in front of peers in a strange accent is a nerve-wracking situation, which is compounded if the students are also worrying about accuracy of grammar, content, or comprehension. If the teacher is aware of strategies and instructional methods to lower the affective filter in his or her students, then this anxiety can be diminished. Consequently, the more students are better able to comprehend content like vocabulary and grammar structures, the more apt they will be to partake in output such as responding to a request in the target language.

Research

"The individual's attitudes to the classroom form an important component in L2 learning. The student's attitudes towards the learning situation, as measured by feelings about the classroom teacher and level of anxiety about the classroom, contribute to the student's motivation"

(Cook, 2008, p. 163).

LOW-STRESS OPPORTUNITIES FOR OUTPUT

Providing comprehensible input alone isn't enough. Students also benefit from low-stress opportunities for output. Please note that this does not mean that we push students beyond where they are emotionally ready to go. As teachers, we need to take appropriate steps to scaffold opportunities in which students feel comfortable taking part in producing new sounds and structures in the target language.

In 1985, Merrill Swain, a Canadian researcher studying the role of language output, or "production," proposed the "Pushed Output Hypothesis." Her research compared L1 (first language) English students schooled in the French immersion models in Canada to students of the same age (K-6) growing up

with French as their L1. The study found that the French language of the first group was not perfectly native-like, even though the schools were full of comprehensible input. While the students' comprehension abilities were comparable, what was lacking were sufficient opportunities for the students "to actually use the language in meaningful ways, through speaking and writing" (Ortega, 2009, p. 62). Swain's research (1985) concludes that output, or language produced by the students is critical for language development. Despite achieving high levels of comprehension in their L2, the French learners were lacking opportunities to produce "extended stretches of French themselves," and thus were not developing native-like proficiency or grammatical accuracy (Gibbons, 2002, p. 15). The language that was produced needed to be more refined, and in order to do this, students needed to be prompted to use a more sophisticated language in meaningful ways.

Swain proposed that "producing the target language may be the trigger that forces the learner to pay attention to the means of expression needed in order to successfully convey his or her own intended meaning" (Swain, 1985, p. 249). The students would receive more fine-tuned and quality feedback if the language being produced was more fine-tuned and comprehensible in and of itself. In order to produce this language, the student must "notice" the gap between this more sophisticated, academic language and his or her own current level. Swain more recently refers to this as "stretched" language, as these situations require the learner to use language beyond what they currently know and can control (Gibbons, 2015).

The goal of a successful language learning experience is for students to receive native-like target language input and (hopefully) produce native-like output. Of course, not all learners will acquire second language features and skills at the same rate even under the same learning conditions, and that's okay (VanPatten & Williams, 2014). Remember, we teachers can't control many of the factors that affect our students' development. What we can do, however, is provide access to the target language while remembering that outcomes will vary from student to student.

While direct instruction is important, the process of second language acquisition involves both formal and informal encounters with the second language (Callahan, Wilkinson, Muller, & Frisco, 2008). The teacher plays a critical role in this equation, for his or her purposeful planning elicits certain target language responses from the students. When students produce incorrect target language responses, the teacher has an opportunity to effectively recast the response for the student. A recast happens when a teacher simply restates a student's incorrect word, utterance, or question in the correct manner in the target language. A teacher does this without changing the meaning of the student's original response or raising the student's affective filter. Recasts have been shown to have a positive impact on second language acquisition (Leeman, 2003).

TEACHER: What class did you just come from?
STUDENT: I come from Biology.
TEACHER: You *came* from Biology. How was Biology? Was it a fun class?
STUDENT: Yes, it was a fun class.

Recasting is a strategy that involves both input and output. It is an important component of teaching in the target language. And while teaching in the target language is important, according to the ACTFL guidelines, it is "necessary but not sufficient for increasing one's proficiency." To clarify, this means that "use of the target language must be accompanied by a variety of strategies to facilitate comprehension and support meaning making. Comprehensible input and comprehensible output go hand-in-hand." Though each of the concepts and theories mentioned above convey important aspects of the SLA experience, they build on one another to both produce an effective language learning environment and to foster a competent second language learner.

Optimal L2 learning must include opportunities for language use that are slightly beyond what the learner currently can handle in speaking or writing, and also production that is meaningful and whose demands exceed the learner's current abilities. By encouraging risk full attempts by the learner to handle complex content beyond current competence, such conditions of language use may drive learning *(Ortega, 2009)*.

Photo courtesy of Frisco ISD

Quality of Instruction

"Everything the teacher does provides the learner with opportunities for encountering the language" (Cook, 2008, p. 164).

Photo courtesy of Frisco ISD

Now for a moment of vulnerability: I had anxiety with speaking French in front of my students. As a non-native speaker and teacher of French, my greatest level of anxiety was in speaking the language with native speakers. The mere notion that native French speakers might notice every mistake I made conjured up a sense of anxiety, coupled with fear of misunderstanding their spoken word. After taking several trips to France (and being understood!), this feeling has slightly subsided. But as a classroom teacher, I initially felt self-conscious when speaking in front of my French foreign language teacher colleagues. My affective filter definitely needed lowering!

In her seminal research, Elaine Horwitz (1986) developed the Foreign Language Classroom Anxiety Scale (FLCAS) as an instrument to measure learners' anxiety, perceptions, and beliefs as they pertained to their related experiences in the foreign language classroom. As a language learner myself, I could completely relate to this, and I could also see how knowledge of this type of anxiety along with learner differences could affect my quality of instruction. Interestingly, on the first day of the second language acquisition class in

my post-graduate program at UT Austin, I was sitting in Dr. Horwitz' class. She not only introduced us to the FLCAS to see how our students may have measured up, but she made us aware that "Teacher Foreign Language Anxiety" existed as an established, researched concept. After her original research with students, she developed a similar measurement tool for teachers to assess their own levels of confidence or anxiety when teaching in this context (Horwitz, 1996; Horwitz, 2013). It was quite reassuring for me to see that other foreign language teachers faced this problem, and I wasn't alone.

> An important element of L2 success appears to be how learners are treated: the teaching method they encounter, the language they hear and the environment in which they are learning. The purpose of language teaching in one sense is to provide optimal samples of language for the learner to profit from – the best 'input' to the process of language learning. Everything the teacher does provides the learners with opportunities for encountering the language
>
> *(Cook, 2008, p. 162).*

My further studies in foreign language education helped me understand the true definition of "fluency" in a second language. To a lay person, the idea of being "fluent" automatically means that you can say absolutely everything in the target language.

As Francois Grosjean (2010) explains, this is simply not the case:

> "If one were to count as bilingual only those people who pass as complete monolinguals in each of their languages (they are a rarity), one would be left with no label for the vast majority of people who use two or more languages regularly but who do not have native-like fluency in each. The reason they don't is quite simply that bilinguals do not need to be equally competent in all of their languages. They usually acquire and use their languages for different purposes, in different domains of life, with different people."

Being able to distinguish that I am sufficiently proficient to be certified by the state to teach French, should have been enough for me to have the confidence to do so without anxiety. As Horwitz stated, "few nonnative teachers will have the necessary time or access to a target language community" to achieve the result of complete "fluency" (1996, p. 367). Thus, recognizing that this feeling of apprehension does exist but giving myself credit for what I have achieved in the target language was a necessary first step for relieving my anxiety.

CTIONAL NORMS

In a high-quality foreign language classroom, students will acquire language at a faster rate than in a classroom of lesser caliber. A high-quality foreign language classroom is one in which the teacher is able to increase student motivation and provide sufficient opportunities for comprehensible input and low-stress opportunities for output. The quality of instruction is a factor that is purely in our control as teachers. We can provide comprehensible input and low-stress opportunities for output for our students. The 7 Steps are designed to help you accomplish those two goals.

THE (7) STEPS TO A
Language-Rich, Interactive Foreign Language Classroom:

1. Teach students what to say when they don't know what to say

2. Have students speak in complete sentences

3. Randomize and rotate when calling on students

4. Use total response signals

5. Use targeted visuals and vocabulary to increase comprehension

6. Have students participate in structured conversations

7. Have students participate in structured reading and writing activities

The 7 Steps aren't so much a methodology, but they are instructional norms that increase the input and low-stress opportunities for output within many methodologies of second language instruction. (For a more complex study of different theories and approaches to second language learning, please refer to the overview found in the Appendix on pg. 172.) An instructional norm can be thought of as a particular routine or activity that you regularly use in teaching to elicit a specific outcome. For example, in my French classroom, students would enter and immediately pick up their interactive notebooks before the bell rang. They would open to their daily warm-up page and copy the sentence stems I had posted in the bottom left corner of my whiteboard. The stems would reflect the previous day's content. It was my "norm" to use this as a tool so that students could produce language that I could then use as a daily formative assessment. Students worked individually or in pairs to complete the stems while I walked around the classroom checking work, answering questions, and rewarding my students with either stamps or checkmarks. For my classroom, this was a daily norm.

Another norm I embraced was pre-teaching vocabulary when starting a new unit by allowing students to view a short video containing the selected words. Using context clues, my students would infer the meaning of these words, especially if no English or Spanish cognates existed to help

them. Another norm I implemented was tied to daily attendance. A different student each day would cycle through the color-coded set of index cards I had created for each class period. This gave the "roll caller" an opportunity to practice his or her French pronunciation. Over time these norms became, for me, "habits" of instruction. The 7 Steps can also become "habits" that are seamlessly incorporated into daily instruction.

COMMUNICATION

These 7 Steps provide a simple road map for the high-quality, foreign language education we want our students to have. Our goal is to create classrooms where every student participates in target language conversations in a low-stress, engaging environment. We want our students to see things from multiple perspectives, and to be able to express themselves intelligently.

Communication is at the heart of foreign language instruction. Bill VanPatten (2014) defines communication in language-learning as the expression and interpretation of meaning in a given context. This is done by engaging in acts of expressing and interpreting meaning in a variety of contexts, which foreign language teachers can provide by interactive activities that foster meaning-making in the target language.

Communicative ability cannot be "drilled." It cannot be practiced in the traditional sense of practice. Communicative ability develops because we find ourselves in communicative contexts. Thus, output (the expression of meaning) plays a major role in the development of communicative ability *(VanPatten, 2014)*.

The 7 Steps can be implemented within the context of ACTFL's "World Readiness Standard of Communication." While it can certainly be integrated into all five goal areas, the most practical fit is in the Communication goal area, and that will be the primary focus of this book. Bill VanPatten (2014) tells us that students' communicative ability happens by engaging in communication. Researchers that chronicle the development of modern second language acquisition theories emphasize the shift to methodologies that support learners' communicative needs being met more effectively than grammar drills and rote memorization (Gass & Selinker, 2008). The strategies in this book, as well as the accompanying activities, are primarily rooted in this communicative method of second language instruction. These include appropriate greetings, gestures, and nonverbal behaviors as well as authentic communication in the target language (Horwitz, 2013).

It is important to note that these strategies are effective for increasing student performance in communicative academic situations, as well as for increasing students' proficiency. ACTFL defines performance as "the ability to use language that has been learned and practiced in an instructional setting." Communicative performance is successful when students have learned the "language functions, structures, and vocabulary they will apply on the assessment tasks," rather than having memorized scripts. As students practice communication strategies in the classroom that allow them to receive comprehensible input, they are also learning strategies that will increase their proficiency. Proficiency is defined by ACTFL as "the ability to use language in real-world situations in a spontaneous interaction and non-rehearsed context and in a manner acceptable and appropriate to native speakers of the language." Without these communication strategies, proficiency is difficult to attain.

The communication standard is outlined here:

II. World Languages Learning Standards

The standards indicate what students should know and be able to do as they study and learn to communicate in a language other than English. There are eleven standards in five goal areas.

1.0 Communication

Communicate effectively in more than one language in order to function in a variety of situations and for multiple purposes.

> **> 1.1 Interpersonal Communication**
> Learners interact and negotiate meaning in spoken, signed, or written conversations to share information, reactions, feelings, and opinions.

> **> 1.2 Interpretive Communication**
> Learners understand, interpret, and analyze what is heard, read, or viewed on a variety of topics.

> **> 1.3 Presentational Communication**
> Learning present information, concepts, and ideas to inform, explain, persuade, and narrate on a variety of topics using appropriate media and adapting to various audiences of listerners, readers, or viewers.

The norms established by the 7 Steps support not only the ACTFL standards of Communication but also other World Language, Foreign Language, or LOTE Communication standards set by most states in the country. The table below refers to comparisons of the 7 Steps to strategies endorsed by ACTFL for supporting target language use during foreign language instruction.

7 Steps to a Language-Rich, Interactive Foreign Language Classroom	ACTFL Suggested Strategies*
PROVIDE A LANGUAGE-RICH ENVIRONMENT	
1. Teach students what to say when they don't know what to say	• Teach students strategies for requesting clarification and assistance when faced with comprehension difficulties • Don't use English (or one's native language) as the default for checking on meaning
2. Have students speak in complete sentences	• Elicit talk that increases in fluency, complexity, and accuracy over time • Negotiate meaning with students, and encourage negotiation among students
3. Randomize and rotate when calling on students	• Conduct comprehension checks to ensure understanding
4. Use total response signals	• Conduct comprehension checks to ensure understanding
5. Use targeted visuals and vocabulary strategies to increase comprehension	• Support comprehension and production through context/gestures/visual support • Focus on meaning before details
6. Have students participate in structured conversations	• Elicit talk that increases in fluency, complexity, and accuracy over time • Negotiate meaning with students, and encourage negotiation among students
7. Have students participate in structured reading/writing activities	• Negotiate meaning with students, and encourage negotiation among students

*Based on https://www.actfl.org/guiding-principles/use-target-language-language-learning/strategies

For the AP® Foreign Language Course Instructor and the IB Diploma Programme Language Acquisition Instructor

Each of the 7 Steps is vital to the creation of a communicative, interactive classroom. Language education must be seen from a "holistic approach" wherein each mode of communication is used to gain and share information. This information can be about the language itself, but it is also used as a tool to share and exchange knowledge. As the AP® Curriculum Framework suggests, there is a "complex interrelatedness of comprehension and comprehensibility, vocabulary usage, language control, communication strategies, and cultural awareness." Teachers must provide opportunities for students to acquire "language structures in context and use them to convey meaning" (College Board, n.d., p.5).

The 7 Steps equip both the teacher and the learner with the tools to exchange information in the target language. By incorporating them into your classroom, you will be equipped to meet AP® course requirements to teach in the target language, and you will be able to provide opportunities for your students to demonstrate proficiency in the target language.

You will also be using the three modes of communication in order to exchange information on Culture, Connections, Comparisons, and Communities as required by the AP® course syllabus and as outlined by ACTFL. Additionally, the IB course description for language acquisition states that "interactive, productive, and receptive skills are developed through contextualized study of language, texts, and themes" (IB Organization, n.d.). Implementation of the 7 Steps can help you to meet these curriculum goals.

The 7 Steps provide strategies and opportunities for students to gain literacy and functional language competence. These 7 Steps will help your students acquire language and become highly proficient in its use, in both academic and real-life situations. AP® Course requirements insist that students be prepared "to use the language in real-life settings" (College Board, n.d., p. 37). Each of the levels of the IB language course description and aims intend "to provide students with a basis for further study, work, and leisure through the use of an additional language and to provide the opportunity for enjoyment, creativity and intellectual stimulation through knowledge of an additional language" (IB Organization, n.d.). In other words, students are acquiring a language so that they may experience the world through a plurality of life experiences, and will not be confined to one culture, language, or perspective on life.

The College Board has established that one of their policies is to provide equity and equal access to education for all students. They "encourage the elimination of barriers that restrict access to AP® for students from ethnic, racial, and socioeconomic groups that have been traditionally underserved" (College Board, n.d., p. ii). This is why it is so important for language educators to consider the things that are in their control and to provide a high standard of quality instruction and access to language, and to share motivating factors that will help to reduce barriers to second language acquisition for all students.

Photo courtesy of Anna Matis

THE *Seven Steps*

Barcelona, Spain

STEP ① *Teach Students What to Say When They Don't Know What to Say*

What is Step 1?

As teachers, we have all been frustrated by calling on students who maintain a long silence as they stare at the floor, shrug their shoulders, and say, "I don't know." This is especially true in the foreign language classroom, in which a healthy mix of anxiety and genuine lack of comprehension can lead to doubt and confusion when it comes to responding to questions. We are all looking for ways to banish, "I don't know," "Huh," and "What," from our classrooms. One solution that works is to teach students to respond differently when they are unsure about an answer to a question. There are specific alternatives that help students get past the "I don't know" stage. Using these alternatives helps create an expectation of accountable conversation.

In working with students from diverse backgrounds, one of the biggest challenges facing us is the phenomenon known as learned helplessness. Sometimes as teachers, we actually train students to be helpless. Every time we ask students to respond to a question or perform a task yet fail to hold them accountable for their response or performance, we send them a message: You are not expected to achieve. By teaching students how to help themselves, we enable them to overcome learned helplessness and really become independent learners. It is not enough just to tell students to think for themselves and try

harder. We have to teach many of our students the language and habits of independent learners so that they can become independent learners. Teaching our students how to acquire helpful information when they are confused and teaching them to think about the steps involved in reaching a specific goal gives them the skills they can use inside and outside of school.

Step 1 involves teaching foreign language learners the communication strategies that will allow them to access new language at an i+1 level. These strategies help them "opt-in" because they provide a means to negotiate meaning and comprehension. Students are empowered with the language chunks that they will practice regularly and that will become a base for them to seek out and understand new language in future contexts, both instructional and authentic.

Here's how it works: We provide a poster for students that lists alternatives to saying "I Don't Know." Classrooms across the country have implemented this strategy in content-area classrooms, especially with ESL students. The phrases below are examples of what would be posted and used in the target language of the foreign language classroom. We will refer to these phrases as "Clarification Stems" throughout the book.

What to Say Instead of "I Don't Know"
CLARIFICATION STEMS

> May I please have some more information?

> May I please have some time to think?

> Would you please repeat the question?

> How do I say _____ in (the target language)?

> How do you pronounce_____in (the target language)?

> I think this means_____.

> May I ask a friend for help?

Que dire au lieu de « Je ne sais pas »

- Pouvez-vous me donner plus d'informations?
- Pouvez-vous me laisser un peu de temps pour réfléchir?
- Pouvez-vous répéter la question s'il vous plaît?
- Comment dit-on _____ en français?
- Comment prononcez-vous _____ en français?
- Je pense que cela signifie _____
- Puis-je demander l'aide d'un ami?

Qué decir en lugar de "No sé"

- ¿Me podría dar más información?
- ¿Me podría dar tiempo para pensar?
- ¿Podría repetir la pregunta?
- ¿Cómo se dice _____ en español?
- ¿Cómo se pronuncia _____en español?
- Creo que esto significa_____
- ¿Podría pedirle ayuda a un compañero?

Was zu sagen anstelle von, "Ich weiß nicht."

- Kann ich bitte mehr Informationen bekommen?
- Kann ich bitte Zeit zum Nachdenken bekommen?
- Können Sie die Frage bitte wiederholen?
- Wie sage ich _____auf Deutsch?
- Wie spreche ich_____auf Deutsch aus?
- Ich denke das bedeutet, _____
- Darf ich eine Freundin/ einen Freund um Hilfe bitten?

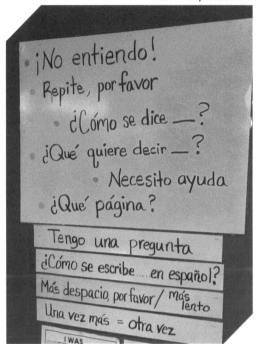

¡No entiendo!

Repite, por favor

¿Cómo se dice ___?

¿Qué quiere decir ___?

Necesito ayuda

¿Qué página?

Tengo una pregunta

¿Cómo se escribe ... en español?

Más despacio, por favor / más lento

Una vez más = otra vez

I WAS

The power of teaching this strategy during these initial days of the course is that students immediately learn very useful phrases in the target language that can stick with them both in and out of the foreign language classroom. When their friends ask them to "say something" in the target language, students can immediately sound smart and respond with a phrase in the form of a complete sentence! An added benefit to this strategy is the upfront expectation that student-teacher interactions will be happening in the target language. A phrase as simple as "May I go to the bathroom?" can reinforce the use of the target language for every student multiple times a week.

After posting the responses, whenever a teacher asks a question, students have two choices: respond to the teacher or request assistance and then respond. Students may use the phrase (in the target language), "I don't know" if they then follow it with one of the Clarification Stems. The important principle is that students must always respond. They might not respond correctly, and they might need some extra time or support, but opting out of the conversation is not an option.

On the first or second day of school, demonstrate how to use the responses, and explain the procedure. Subsequently, all students are responsible for participating. After modeling the way to use the responses, explain what is meant by the expectation of accountable conversation.

After initially introducing the expectation of accountable conversation to students and using the poster of alternative responses in the classroom, we are ready to branch out and teach students what to say when they don't know what to say in other ways. The basic idea is to give students specific sentences and questions to use in different situations so that they can independently seek help when they need it.

Imagine a teacher and student having a conversation in the target language. It might sound something like the following:

Language isn't something you do on your own.

English

TEACHER Emmanuel, what did you do last night?

EMMANUEL *(looking confused):* I don't know.

TEACHER *(gesturing to poster/stems):* Can you use one of our stems?

EMMANUEL How do I say, "I studied last night" in *(target language)*?

TEACHER You say "J'ai étudié hier soir." Class, can you please repeat this phrase?

CLASS *(chorally responds):* J'ai étudié hier soir.

TEACHER So Emmanuel, what did you do last night?

EMMANUEL J'ai étudié hier soir.

French

TEACHER Emmanuel, qu'as-tu fait hier soir?

EMMANUEL *(looking confused):* I don't know.

TEACHER *(gesturing to poster/stems):* Peux-tu utiliser une de nos phrases-type?

EMMANUEL Comment dit-on "I studied last night" en français?

TEACHER On dit : « J'ai étudié hier soir ». Classe, pouvez-vous répéter cette phrase, s'il-vous-plaît?

CLASS (chorally responds): J'ai étudié hier soir.

TEACHER Donc, Emmanuel, qu'as-tu fait hier soir?

EMMANUEL J'ai étudié hier soir.

Spanish

TEACHER Emmanuel, ¿qué hiciste anoche?

EMMANUEL *(looking confused):* I don't know.

TEACHER *(gesturing to poster/stems):* ¿Puedes utilizar uno de los fragmentos del cartel?

EMMANUEL ¿Cómo se dice "I studied last night" en español?

TEACHER Se dice: "Estudié anoche." Clase, ¿pueden repetir esta frase?

CLASS (chorally responds): Estudié anoche.

TEACHER Entonces, Emmanuel, ¿qué hiciste anoche?

EMMANUEL Estudié anoche.

TEACHER Emmanuel, was hast du gestern Abend gemacht?

EMMANUEL *(looking confused)*: I don't know.

TEACHER *(gesturing to poster/stems)*: Kannst du einen unserer Satzstämme verwenden?

EMMANUEL Wie sage ich, "I studied last night" auf Deutsch?

TEACHER Man sagt: "Ich habe gestern Abend gelernt." Könnt ihr diesen Satz alle zusammen wiederholen?

CLASS (chorally responds): Ich habe gestern Abend gelernt.

TEACHER Also Emmanuel, was hast du gestern Abend gemacht?

EMMANUEL Ich habe gestern Abend gelernt.

For the AP® Foreign Language Course Instructor and the IB Diploma Programme Language Acquisition Instructor

It is essential to incorporate these strategies in foreign language instruction for all students. Novice students who learn how to acquire a second language will progress faster in their communicative abilities if they have a strong base of communication strategies. However, teaching intermediate and advanced students these strategies is key to their success in rigorous courses such as those designed to help them pass the AP® or the IB tests. The AP® test is designed with college-level expectations in mind, and both teachers and students are expected to "meet or exceed" those expectations (College Board, n.d., p.2). The lowest score that a student can receive on the AP® test is a 0 (unacceptable). This score reflects responses that are "mere restatement of language from the prompts, clearly does not respond to the prompts, 'I don't know,' 'I don't understand' or equivalent in any language, not in the language of the exam, or blank" (College Board, n.d., p. 97). Step 1 is the first step in moving your students from an unacceptable level of language proficiency to a "well qualified" (4) or "extremely well-qualified" (5) score of language proficiency as required by the College Board (College Board, n.d., p.4

OES STEP 1 PROVIDE STUDENTS WITH ATION AND ACCESS TO LANGUAGE?

Motivation

☐ **Lowering the affective filter:** Implementing this step as a classroom norm actually lowers the affective filter for students in the room. At first it will feel like a game, and students will generally be enthusiastic about providing alternative responses to the "I don't know" that has become such a classic phrase in their repertoire. As it develops into a norm, students who are reluctant to respond to new questions can take comfort in knowing that an academic response, along with guiding questions in the target language, is always at their fingertips.

☐ **Creating a culture of mutual support:** I encourage teachers to embed this strategy into their classroom culture and to encourage accountability from both the teacher and students to adhere to its use. This way all students, even our reluctant ones, will be supported in their ability to respond in the target language — even if they don't know the correct response to the teacher's question.

☐ **Encouraging production despite student's individual language proficiency or knowledge of the topic being discussed:** The strategy functions as an encouraging "No Opt Out," a key idea in Doug Lemov's *Teach Like a Champion* (2010). Even if students do not know an answer, they can use one of the Clarification Stems (see pg. 40), and after another classmate has responded correctly, the teacher can return to the original student to repeat the correct answer. Using this strategy demonstrates to students that it is okay to make mistakes or not know an answer, but it is not okay not to try.

☐ **Reducing teacher anxiety when calling on students:** As mentioned before (pg. 30), teachers can have anxiety in their role in speaking and asking questions just as much as students can have anxiety about responding. Dr. Elaine Horwitz's research (1986) addresses both of these issues. The Clarification Stems in Step 1 provide all speakers in the classroom with encouraging phrases to reduce foreign language anxiety in the classroom.

Access to Language

☐ **Encouraging students' first steps into the language:** Since the nature of Step 1 serves as an introduction to the target language and should be one of the first topics of instruction, the phrases immediately provide insight and access to language production and pronunciation from day one.

☐ **Providing opportunities for negotiated input:** This is where the meaning making happens. Students hear words or phrases from the teacher that they may not understand, but the Clarification Stems offer students a tool to help clarify and negotiate for meaning.

☐ **Using accessible language to learn new language:** The beauty of the Clarification Stem responses lies in the fact that students need not revert to English phrases such as, "What does that mean?" or "How do you say that in English?" when they are stuck. They can use the accessible target-language phrases at their fingertips to learn the new language.

What else does research show
about the effectiveness of teaching students what to say when they don't know what to say?

Teaching students what to say when they don't know what to say is a metacognitive strategy. Research on language learners and learning strategies concludes that all learners benefit from the use of metacognitive strategies to monitor and evaluate their own thinking (Chamot, 2004). Countless studies show that the use of metacognitive strategies in the classroom has a positive impact on student performance. For instance, Duffy, (2002), McLaughlin, (2003), Snow, Griffin & Burns (2005), and Vogt & Nagano (2003) discuss the power of teaching students specific strategies to purposefully monitor their own thinking/understanding and choosing a way to access help.

Similarly, Lipson and Wixson (2008) argue that teachers need to teach metacognitive strategies to students, model each strategy, and explain when and why each strategy should be used. Essentially, teachers first show students what to say instead of "I don't know." Then teachers show students how to use various responses. Finally, teachers demonstrate when and why students use the responses.

In her formative book, *Teaching Language in Context*, Alice Omaggio Hadley notes that communication strategies that serve to negotiate meaning can be extremely valuable in the language acquisition process and can contribute to the development of the learners' strategic competence. Of particular importance are the use of paraphrasing strategies and appeals for assistance, as these can offer learners new expressions, structures, and vocabulary to successfully add to their repertoire. Hadley tells us,

"Teachers need to help learners develop their strategic competence through classroom activities that focus on using circumlocution, definitions, and other paraphrasing techniques that lead to successful communication of meaning. Expressions in the target language, such as 'I don't know', 'Could you please repeat that?' or 'Could you please speak more slowly?' can also be taught overtly so that students can appeal for assistance when it is needed" (2001, p. 262).

Of particular importance are the kinds of interactions that occur as speakers clarify their intended meaning, such as when speakers have an opportunity to negotiate and reword what they are trying to say (Gibbons, 2002, p.15).

Teaching and practicing communication strategies with students empowers them to become autonomous learners. In research conducted by Bill Holden and Miyuki Usuki, learner autonomy was linked to increased student success at learning languages, "Autonomous learners are both cognitively and metacognitively aware of their role in the learning process, seek to create their own opportunities to learn, monitor their learning, and attempt actively to manage their learning in and out of the classroom" (Holden & Usuki, 1999, p.18). Negotiating meaning, practicing repetition and iteration, and noticing language use and misuse give control, power, and autonomy to the learner.

FAQ
FREQUENTLY ASKED QUESTIONS

Barcelona, Spain

WHAT IF MY STUDENTS DON'T FEEL COMFORTABLE USING THE CLARIFICATION STEMS?

When trying the strategy for the first time, there are some tips teachers can use to mitigate students' hesitation to speak in the target language, especially if pronunciation is a challenge. Students can hold up a premade response card with the printed phrase. If you don't have a class set, students can easily make them using index cards, which offers writing practice in the target language as well. Also, we can't underestimate the power of choral response. Having the whole class repeat the desired phrase together is a wonderful scaffold that helps lower the affective filter while raising students' comfort with the phraseology. Lastly, during both the initial learning of the phrases or in subsequent requests for more information, teachers can write (or rewrite) the phonetic spelling or pronunciation of words for students to increase their comprehension.

HOW MUCH INFORMATION SHOULD I GIVE WHEN STUDENTS ASK FOR HELP?

The goal is for students to participate as independent learners, so give only the information required to accomplish that goal. We want to support students, not enable them. Scaffolding is support that leads to independence. Enabling is support that leads to dependence. Sometimes specific situations dictate when we might need to give most, or all, of the information to a student to get a response. These include: absence the day before, lack of understanding of current topic or language, or a severe learning disability.

For other learning situations, our focus is to give students the tools to answer questions without help. We might tell a student, "Look in your notes, and I'll get back to you in a minute," or "Let me give you a minute to think, and I'll get back to you." Sometimes when a student asks for help, we can simply reword or rephrase the question in simpler terms so they will be able to respond. We scaffold with the goal that learners will be able to comprehend vocabulary, texts, and tasks without any assistance in the future. Gibbons relates linguistic scaffolding to the scaffolds used during the construction of a building. Scaffolding is temporary, "but essential for the successful construction of the building" (2015, p. 16).

HOW MUCH TIME SHOULD I GIVE STUDENTS WHEN THEY ASK FOR TIME TO THINK?

It's easiest to have students let us know when they have had enough time. This can be accomplished by asking for a specific signal to show they are ready, like saying, "Show me a thumbs up as soon as you're ready," or "Close your book when you're ready to respond." You can read more on the effectiveness of total response signals in Step 4 on p. 86. After a student has asked for time, always be sure they are ready before calling on them. This eliminates the potential for embarrassing a student who isn't ready. If a student still needs help, we can walk over to the desk and provide one-on-one support. Another alternative is to allow students to talk to each other in a think, pair, share exercise (see pg. 132) so that the student who needs more time can get input from his or her peers before responding.

WILL THIS STRATEGY BECOME A CRUTCH FOR STUDENTS WHO OVERUSE IT?

It could if we don't remain focused on accountability and independent learning as the goal. Gradually withdrawing the support we provide when students use the strategy is key. We want to be careful, however, about being too quick to judge students' motives, because they may need more assistance than we think they do. When it appears that a student is always asking for help before responding independently, we can say, "I think you can find out on your own. Look in your notes, and I'll call on you when you show me a thumbs-up." A benefit to the teacher is that students are constantly practicing output in the target language by using the Clarification Stems.

WHAT DO YOU DO WITH THE STUDENT WHO ABSOLUTELY REFUSES TO RESPOND?

Early on, some students may be embarrassed to use a new strategy for fear of looking awkward in front of their peers. This is especially true in the foreign language classroom, where the affective filter may be raised and students are self-conscious about their accents and pronunciation in the target language. When they realize that everyone will be required to use the target language in class from day one, it becomes easier for them to participate. If students are shy, we can have them repeat after us or speak softly at first so that only the teacher can hear them. It is also important to pinpoint why a reluctant student is not willing to respond. Sometimes we may think students are being noncompliant when they simply don't understand what we are asking them to do, or they didn't hear the question.

The easiest way to get our noncompliant students to use alternatives to "I don't know" is to act as if they plan to participate. Just smile politely and respectfully, and ask them, "Please use one of these Clarification Stems." Then wait. If they flatly refuse, model the strategy and then ask again, letting tone and body language communicate the expectation that they will participate. If they still refuse to participate, then it's time to look at other options: a private conference with the student, finding out if there are other issues at play, or moving ahead with another classroom management system already in place.

WON'T SOME STUDENTS ALWAYS ASK A FRIEND FOR HELP AND THEN BECOME TOO DEPENDENT ON OTHERS?

It can be helpful to depend on a peer for extended support while learning a new language. If a student consistently uses a phrase in the target language like, "May I ask a friend for help?" and we believe they can be more independent, we say (in English or the target language), "I think you know this. Why don't you think about it for just a minute, and I'll get back to you." If we see that support is still needed, we can walk to the desk and provide one-on-one support, or we can direct them to resources that can provide information. Interestingly, sometimes hearing another student model the foreign language can be just what a struggling student needs to progress in proficiency.

WHAT ABOUT STUDENTS WITH SPECIAL NEEDS, DO THEY HAVE TO RESPOND AS WELL?

As a general rule, we have found that all students can follow the accountability rule. If a student's individualized education plan or disability makes it impossible for them to participate, adjustments are needed. We want to be very careful here. Many times, students are capable of more than we imagine when they are given a chance.

FAQ CONTINUED

WILL THESE STRATEGIES SLOW DOWN MY INSTRUCTION AS I PROVIDE ASSISTANCE FOR STRUGGLING LEARNERS?

When we start to apply the expectation of accountable conversation, it could slow down instruction, especially when students are just getting used to both the procedure and the foreign language! Students often struggle as they try to master thinking independently and as they become responsible for learning. Many of our students have never been expected to participate in class discussions, or they are rarely held accountable for responding orally in class. Expect it to take some time for students to adjust and feel safe responding.

Even when we carefully monitor our pacing and thoughtfully plan the curriculum, we may struggle with effective ways to handle a student's requests for more information. One strategy that benefits students, keeps the pace of the lesson, and still provides support is "Turn and Tell Five" (see pg. 54). Here's how it works: When we call on a student, and the student requests more information, we tell the whole class to turn to the person next to them and discuss possible answers. Students are given five seconds to speak to one another. We then call on the same student who requested information and give them an opportunity to respond.

Take a look at this sample dialogue between a classroom teacher and student:

TEACHER Pablo, what is this newspaper article about?

PABLO I don't know.

(Teacher points to the poster with clarification stems.)

PABLO Oh… Can I please have some more information?

TEACHER Sure, everyone talk to your partner for about 5 seconds about what the article was about.

(Teacher walks over to Pablo's desk, listens to make sure that Pablo's partner is able to clarify the answer. His partner tells him the article was about school lunches in France).

TEACHER *(speaking quietly to Pablo)* Pablo, can you repeat that for me?

PABLO Yeah...the article was about school lunches in France.

TEACHER Good. Okay class, let me get your attention *(speaking in front of whole class)*. Pablo, can you tell me what the article is about?

PABLO Yes, the article is about school lunches in France.

TEACHER Thank you, Pablo.

TEACHER Pablo, de quoi parle cet article de journal?

PABLO I don't know.

(Teacher points to the poster with clarification stems.)

PABLO Euh... Puis-je avoir plus d'informations?

TEACHER Bien sûr! Je vous invite à discuter avec votre voisin pendant environ 5 secondes pour identifier le sujet de l'article.

(Teacher walks over to Pablo's desk, listens to make sure that Pablo's partner is able to clarify the answer. His partner tells him the article was about school lunches in France).

TEACHER *(speaking quietly to Pablo)* Pablo, peux-tu répéter ce que ton camarade vient de dire?

PABLO Oui... l'article parlait des repas scolaires en France.

TEACHER Bien! Ok tout le monde, écoutez Pablo! *(speaking in front of whole class).* Peux-tu me dire de quoi parle l'article?

PABLO Oui, l'article parle des repas scolaires en France.

TEACHER Merci, Pablo.

TEACHER Pablo, ¿de qué se trata este artículo periodístico?

PABLO I don't know.

(Teacher points to the poster with clarification stems.)

PABLO Oh... ¿Me puede dar un poco más de información?

TEACHER Claro, hablen con su compañero por 5 segundos de lo que trata el artículo.

(Teacher walks over to Pablo's desk, listens to make sure that Pablo's partner is able to clarify the answer. His partner tells him the article was about school lunches in France).

TEACHER *(speaking quietly to Pablo)* Pablo, ¿puedes repetir eso?

PABLO Claro. . . el artículo era sobre los almuerzos escolares en Francia.

TEACHER Bien. Bien clase, necesito su atención *(speaking in front of whole class).* Pablo, ¿puedes decirme de qué se trata el artículo?

PABLO Sí, el artículo es sobre los almuerzos escolares en Francia.

TEACHER Gracias, Pablo.

TEACHER Pablo, worum geht es in dem Zeitungsartikel?

PABLO I don't know.

(Teacher points to the poster with clarification stems.)

PABLO Oh... kann ich bitte mehr Informationen bekommen?

TEACHER Sicher, jeder kann mit seinem Partner für 5 Sekunden besprechen, worum es in dem Artikel geht.

(Teacher walks over to Pablo's desk, listens to make sure that Pablo's partner is able to clarify the answer. His partner tells him the article was about school lunches in France).

TEACHER *(speaking quietly to Pablo)* Pablo, kannst du das für mich wiederholen?

PABLO Ja,... in dem Artikel geht es um das Mittagessen an französischen Schulen.

TEACHER Gut. Okay, alle zusammen, passt auf *(speaking in front of whole class).* Pablo, kannst du mir sagen, worum es in dem Artikel geht?

PABLO Ja, in dem Artikel geht es um das Mittagessen an französischen Schulen.

TEACHER Danke, Pablo.

Step 1 ACTIVITIES

1. Banish "I Don't Know"

DESCRIPTION

Many students have grown accustomed to answering teacher questions by saying, "I don't know." In fact, all too often, this is a student's first response, and the reasons for the response are varied. Sometimes students really don't know the answer to the question; other times, they just don't feel comfortable speaking in the target language. Too often, teachers accept an "I don't know" response and quickly move on to another student or offer the answer themselves. This practice trains students to be helpless and passive, and it communicates this idea: "You are not expected to communicate in the target language." Instead of accepting an "I don't know" response, teachers can hold students accountable for responding in another, more productive way. When students are taught specific response phrases, such as our suggested Clarification Stems (see pg. 40), they begin to move away from being helpless and passive to being independent and engaged in the classroom.

DIRECTIONS

1. Create a large poster that lists alternatives to saying "I don't know" in the target language. Review each line of the poster with students.

2. Tell students that saying "I don't know" stands in the way of learning. Explain that "I don't know" is an obstacle that can be moved. Tell students they can refer to the poster for a response that will direct them toward learning the target language, instead of away from it.

3. Tell students they have two choices when you ask them a question: they can respond, or they can request assistance by using one question from the poster. Either way, students must respond to questions in the target language without using "I don't know."

4. Give specific examples of how to use the questions on the poster. For example, note the types of additional information you might provide, model think-aloud methods, show how to check with a classmate, or point to the resources within the classroom where students can find help.

5. Point to the poster when students give an "I don't know" response to a question. Be sure to hold students accountable during class discussions for responding without using "I don't know."

(Adapted from Seidlitz & Perryman, 2011)

2. "I Don't Know" Game

DESCRIPTION

This activity helps students build vocabulary by using communication stems focused on gathering information related to a topic or word. Similar to the game "20 Questions," students use words and phrases in the target language to try to guess a "secret" word selected by the teacher.

DIRECTIONS

1. On the board, create three columns: Clues, Words/Phrases, and Sentences. This chart will be used to track information the students provide during the game.

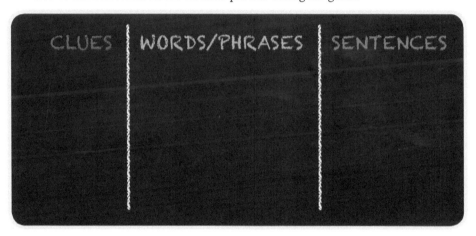

2. Introduce students to the Clarification Stems (see pg. 40).

3. Select a word in the target language.

4. Explain to the students the following rules of the game:
   a. Each student may ask up to two questions per turn.
   b. All questions must be asked in the target language.
   c. Students may use the Clarification Stems, dictionaries, and electronic resources during the activity.
   d. The teacher will not speak English during the game.
   e. If the students guess the word within 20 questions, they win.

5. Give students one clue to start them off (e.g., "It is a person," "It is a place," or "It is a thing.")

6. Record correct and incorrect student responses in the column labeled "Clues," record all new words and phrases students use in the "Words/Phrases" column, and record any new sentences students use in the "Sentences" column.

7. Review pronunciation of words and phrases used.

OPTIONAL ⟶ *Give a short, ungraded quiz on words and phrases used*

Step 1 ACTIVITIES

3. Clarification Game

DESCRIPTION

This is a strategy for introducing students to the Clarification Stems (see pg. 40).

DIRECTIONS

1. Introduce the Clarification Stems to students by explaining that students will use these instead of saying "I don't know" or "Huh?" or using English to ask for clarification.

2. Model correct pronunciation of the stems, and have students repeat.

3. Provide opportunities for students to practice pronouncing the stems with a partner or in small groups.

4. Model expected use of the stems.

5. Provide opportunities for students to practice using the stems individually in a whole-class setting.

    a. Have the students write their names on index cards, and collect the cards.

    b. Teach students how to say the following phrases:

My name is... His/Her name is... Your name is...	Je m'appelle... Il / Elle s'appelle... Tu t'appelles...
Mi nombre es... Su nombre es... Tu nombre es...	Ich heiße... Er/sie heißt... Du heißt...

    c. Tell the students that you will only be using the target language for the next five minutes.

    d. Explain to the students that they are only allowed to speak in the target language as well, unless they are asking a fellow student for help.

    e. Speak to the students in the target language and randomly select students to respond using the deck of index cards with students' names.

f. Ask the students questions such as the following:

What is your name?	Comment t'appelles-tu?
What is his/her name?	Comment s'appelle-t-il / elle?
What is my name?	Quel est mon nom?
What letter does your name start with?	Quelle est la première lettre de ton prénom?
What is your last name?	Quel est ton nom de famille?

¿Cómo te llamas?	**Wie heißt du?**
¿Cómo se llama?	**Wie heißt er/sie?**
¿Cómo me llamo?	**Wie heiße ich?**
¿Con qué letra empieza tu nombre?	**Mit welchem Buchstaben beginnt dein Name?**
¿Cuál es tu apellido?	**Wie lautet dein Nachname?**

g. Occasionally ask the students a question they might not know the answer to — or not know how to respond to — allowing them to use the Clarification Stems. For example, "What letter does your name start with?" or "What is your last name?".

h. Have students use the stems, and provide support to model correct use of the stems.

EXTENSION ⟶ *Play again using a different topic in a few weeks.*

Step 1 ACTIVITIES

4. Turn and Tell Five

DESCRIPTION

This strategy benefits students by offering the support of their peers to clarify or negotiate meaning when they are unsure how to respond orally in class. Students are not only receiving wait time, but the chance to discuss answers with a partner lowers the affective filter and can remove barriers to target-language output, such as nerves and anxiety as well as lack of clarity in the correct response.

DIRECTIONS

1. When we call on a student, and the student requests more information, we tell the whole class to turn to the person next to them and discuss possible answers.

2. Students are given five seconds to speak to one another.

3. We then call on the same student who requested information and give him or her an opportunity to respond in the target language.

4. Teachers can also ask students to rotate to new speaking partners in an effort to give students exposure to different models of language from their peers.

Here's an example of how this might sound in a typical classroom:

TEACHER Yesterday, we were learning about how to describe our homes. Can anyone remember the name for a room in your house? Let's see ...*(Teacher draws the name "Luis" out of a stack of cards)* Luis?

LUIS I forgot.

TEACHER Can you use the strategy we talked about earlier? Remember the poster?

LUIS Oh yeah. Can I please have some more information?

TEACHER Sure, Luis. Everyone turn to your partners and give an example of the name of a room in your house; you have five seconds. I'm going to count down with my fingers. Ready, go! (Teacher uses his/her fingers to count from five to one, then speaks to Luis directly) Luis, are you ready?

LUIS Yeah.

TEACHER Okay, everybody, eyes on me. Luis, can you give me an example of a room in a house?

LUIS Yeah, the dining room, right?

TEACHER Yes, great example! Let's see who will be picked to give me another example.

(Adapted from Seidlitz & Perryman, 2011)

TEACHER Hier, on apprenait à décrire nos maisons. Souvenez-vous les salles de la maison? Voyons… *(Teacher draws the name "Luis" out of a stack of cards)* Luis?

LUIS J'ai oublié.

TEACHER Peux-tu utiliser une de nos stratégies dont on a parlé tout à l'heure? Souvenez-vous de l'affiche.

LUIS Ah, oui. Pouvez-vous me donner plus d'informations?

TEACHER Bien sûr, Luis. Tout le monde, tournez-vous vers votre voisin et donnez un exemple d'une salle de la maison; vous avez 5 secondes. Je vais faire le compte à rebours. Allez, C'est parti!
(Teacher uses his/her fingers to count from five to one, then speaks to Luis directly) Luis, tu es prêt à partager?

LUIS Oui.

TEACHER Ok, tout le monde, regardez-moi. Luis, peux-tu nous donner un exemple d'une salle de la maison?

LUIS Oui, la salle à manger, n'est-ce pas?

TEACHER Oui, excellent exemple! Voyons qui sera choisi pour me donner un autre exemple.

TEACHER Ayer estuvimos aprendiendo cómo describir nuestros hogares. ¿Alguien puede recordar el nombre de una habitación en la casa? Veamos… *(Teacher draws the name "Luis" out of a stack of cards)* ¿Luis?

LUIS Me olvidé.

TEACHER ¿Puedes utilizar la estrategia sobre la que hablamos anteriormente? ¿Recuerdas el póster?

LUIS Oh sí. ¿Me puede brindar un poco más de información?

TEACHER Seguro, Luis. Todos diríjanse hacia sus compañeros y brinden un ejemplo del nombre de una habitación en su casa; tienen cinco segundos. Voy a contar con los dedos. ¡Listo, ya! *(Teacher uses his/her fingers to count from five to one, then speaks to Luis directly)* Luis, ¿estás listo?

LUIS Claro.

TEACHER Bien, todos mírenme. Luis, ¿puedes darme un ejemplo de una habitación en la casa?

LUIS Sí, el comedor, ¿está bien?

TEACHER Sí, ¡excelente ejemplo! Veamos a quién más elegiremos para que dé otro ejemplo.

TEACHER Gestern haben wir gelernt unser Zuhause zu beschreiben. Erinnert sich jemand an den Begriff für einen Raum Zuhause? Mal sehen…*(Teacher draws the name "Luis" out of a stack of cards)* Luis?

LUIS Ich vergaß.

TEACHER Kannst du die Strategie benutzen, über die wir früher gesprochen haben? Erinnerst du dich an das Poster?

LUIS Oh, ja. Kann ich bitte mehr Informationen bekommen?

TEACHER Sicher, Luis. Dreht euch alle zu euren Partnern und gebt ein Beispiel für einen Raum in eurem Zuhause; ihr habt fünf Sekunden. Ich werde die Zeit an meinen Fingern abzählen. Fertig, los! *(Teacher uses his/her fingers to count from five to one, then speaks to Luis directly)* Luis, bist du bereit?

LUIS Ja.

TEACHER Okay, an alle, seht mich an. Luis, kannst du mir ein Beispiel für einen Raum in deinem Zuhause nennen?

LUIS Ja, das Esszimmer, richtig?

TEACHER Ja, gutes Beispiel! Mal sehen wer uns ein anderes Beispiel nennen kann.

Photo courtesy of Anna Matis

Berlin, Germany

STEP ② *Have Students Speak in Complete Sentences*

What is Step 2?

Using complete sentences dramatically changes the quality and tone of a foreign language classroom because it helps students become increasingly more comfortable using the target language for expression. One way to support students as they learn to respond with complete sentences in the target language is to provide them with a sentence stem. A sentence stem is a short phrase that gives students part of a sentence and helps them structure a response. This strategy helps students form complete sentences, and it allows students to grow accustomed to the kinds of words and phrases usually found in the target language. Most importantly, however, sentence stems give students an opportunity to practice using new vocabulary words and terms in context.

Sentence stems provide a framework for students to gradually use increasing amounts of the target language. When our students have opportunities to practice using the words and phrases they will encounter in authentic texts and conversations, they are better prepared for those linguistic encounters because the language used is familiar to them. By strategically using general and specific sentence stems, we change the way students talk. When we change the way they talk, we open the door to new ways of thinking.

Imagine the following dialogue:

TEACHER What is one object you would probably find in your backpack?

FELICIA A pen.

TEACHER Correct, you would probably find a pen in your backpack. What else would you find in your backpack?

SHELDON Books.

TEACHER Correct, you would probably find books in your backpack. What else would you find?

MOHAMMED Paper.

TEACHER Correct, you would probably find paper in your backpack.

Now look at the same dialogue but with the addition of sentence stems.

TEACHER What is one object you would probably find in your backpack?

FELICIA I would probably find a pen in my backpack.

TEACHER Correct, you would probably find a pen in your backpack. Can you ask Sheldon what he would probably find in his backpack?

FELICIA Yes, of course. Sheldon, what is one object you would probably find in your backpack?

SHELDON I would probably find books in my backpack.

TEACHER Correct, you would probably find books in your backpack. Can you ask Mohammed what he would probably find in his backpack?

SHELDON Mohammed, what is one object you would probably find in your backpack?

MOHAMMED I would probably find paper in my backpack.

TEACHER Correct Mohammed, you would probably find paper in your backpack.

Without sentence stems:

TEACHER Quel objet peut-on probablement trouver dans ton sac à dos?

FELICIA Un stylo.

TEACHER Correct, on peut certainement trouver un stylo dans ton sac à dos. Que peut-on trouver d'autre dans ton sac à dos?

SHELDON Des livres.

TEACHER Correct, on peut certainement trouver des livres dans ton sac à dos. Que peut-on y trouver d'autre?

MOHAMMED Du papier.

TEACHER Correct, on peut certainement trouver du papier dans ton sac à dos.

TEACHER ¿Qué objeto encontrarías probablemente en tu mochila?

FELICIA Un bolígrafo.

TEACHER Correcto, probablemente encontrarías un bolígrafo en tu mochila. ¿Qué más encontrarías en tu mochila?

SHELDON Libros.

TEACHER Correcto, probablemente encontrarías libros en tu mochila. ¿Qué más encontrarías?

MOHAMMED Papel.

TEACHER Correcto, probablemente encontrarías papel en tu mochila.

TEACHER Welcher Gegenstand befindet sich wahrscheinlich in deinem Rucksack?

FELICIA Ein Stift.

TEACHER Richtig, in deinem Rucksack befindet sich wahrscheinlich ein Stift. Was sonst befindet sich in deinem Rucksack?

SHELDON Bücher.

TEACHER Richtig, in deinem Rucksack befindet sich wahrscheinlich Bücher. Was befindet sich sonst noch?

MOHAMMED Papier.

TEACHER Richtig, in deinem Rucksack befindet sich wahrscheinlich Papier.

With sentence stems:

TEACHER Quel objet peut-on probablement trouver dans ton sac à dos?

FELICIA On peut certainement trouver un stylo dans mon sac à dos.

TEACHER Correct, on peut certainement trouver un stylo dans ton sac à dos. Peux-tu demander à Sheldon ce qu'il pourrait certainement trouver dans son sac à dos?

FELICIA Oui, bien sûr. Sheldon, quel objet peut-on probablement trouver dans ton sac à dos?

SHELDON On peut certainement trouver des livres dans mon sac à dos.

TEACHER Correct, on peut certainement trouver des livres dans ton sac à dos. Peux-tu demander à Mohammed ce qu'il pourrait certainement trouver dans son sac à dos?

SHELDON Mohammed, quel objet peut-on probablement trouver dans ton sac à dos?

MOHAMMED On peut certainement trouver du papier dans mon sac à dos.

TEACHER ¿Qué objeto encontrarías probablemente en tu mochila?

FELICIA Probablemente encontraría un bolígrafo en mi mochila.

TEACHER Correcto, probablemente encontrarías un bolígrafo en tu mochila. ¿Puedes preguntarle a Sheldon qué es lo que probablemente encontraría en su mochila?

FELICIA Sí, por supuesto. Sheldon, ¿qué objeto encontrarías probablemente en tu mochila?

SHELDON Probablemente encontraría libros en mi mochila.

TEACHER Correcto, probablemente encontrarías libros en tu mochila. ¿Puedes preguntarle a Mohammed qué es lo que probablemente encontraría en su mochila?

SHELDON Mohammed, ¿qué objeto encontrarías probablemente en tu mochila?

MOHAMMED Probablemente encontraría papel en mi mochila.

TEACHER Welcher Gegenstand befindet sich wahrscheinlich in deinem Rucksack?

FELICIA In meinem Rucksack befindet sich wahrscheinlich ein Stift.

TEACHER Richtig, in deinem Rucksack befindet sich wahrscheinlich ein Stift. Kannst du Sheldon fragen, was sich wahrscheinlich in seinem Rucksack befindet?

FELICIA Ja, natürlich. Sheldon, welcher Gegenstand befindet sich wahrscheinlich in deinem Rucksack?

SHELDON In meinem Rucksack befinden sich wahrscheinlich Bücher.

TEACHER Richtig, in deinem Rucksack befinden sich wahrscheinlich Bücher. Kannst du Mohammed fragen, was sich wahrscheinlich in seinem Rucksack befindet?

SHELDON Mohammed, welcher Gegenstand befindet sich wahrscheinlich in deinem Rucksack?

MOHAMMED In meinem Rucksack befindet sich wahrscheinlich Papier.

Even though not every single interaction in the classroom requires complete sentences, we want to establish a habit of using complete sentences. In fact, speaking in complete sentences is only the beginning. It is helpful if we encourage our students to share more than just one complete sentence. Additionally, it is very important to provide ample opportunities in class for students to use complete sentences in oral communication. In doing so, students learn how to develop their thoughts and use formal language structures.

It is very hard for students to write in a way they cannot speak. By providing students with opportunities to communicate more fluidly, we give them the gift of comfort in the target language and a passport to communicate in the global world. The beginning of the process is learning to communicate our thoughts completely in a new language by using complete sentences. Some teachers find it helpful to have a specific place in the classroom to post stems that are used frequently or that are going to be used in a particular lesson. This place can be referred to as the "stem wall" and can include stems such as the following:

This simple expectation dramatically improves the quality of interactions in our classroom. When we encourage our students to use complete sentences, they think in complete thoughts in the new language. They link new words to new language structures and are able to practice full sentences in the new language. They are also immediately required to communicate in all modes and to quickly move from a novice to an intermediate range of communication. We can see this represented in the ACTFL Can-Do Statements Proficiency Benchmarks. The movement from Novice to Intermediate is the difference between communicating with practiced and memorized simple sentences to participating in a conversation by creating sentences.

I see...	Je trouve...	Ya veo...	Ich sehe...
I would see...	Je verrais...	Vería ...	Ich würde... sehen.
I like...	J'aime...	Me gusta ...	Ich mag...
I would like...	J'aimerais...	Me gustaría...	Ich würde gern.../ Ich möchte...
I think...	Je pense...	Creo...	Ich denke...

For the AP® Foreign Language Course Instructor and the IB Diploma Programme Language Acquisition Instructor

Teaching students to speak in complete sentences builds fluency and literacy in a language. This fluency carries over from written competence to spoken competence. Students are assessed on their level of language acquisition in each of the modes of communication. Specifically in the spoken and written presentational mode of communication, the ACTFL Performance Standards, Proficiency Benchmarks, Can-Do Statements, and the AP® Exam reflect a higher level of expected literacy. In each of the achievement-level descriptions for Interpersonal and Presentational spoken and written communication for the AP® Exam, level 5 scores are awarded to those students who "use a variety of simple and compound sentences and some complex sentences" (College Board, n.d., p. 9, 13, 22, 26).

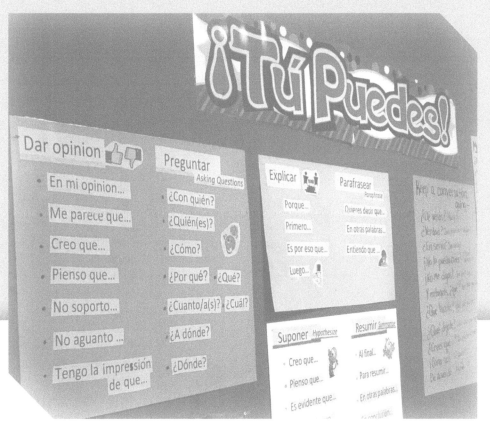

Photo courtesy of Lamar CISD

HOW DOES STEP 2 PROVIDE STUDENTS WITH MOTIVATION AND ACCESS TO LANGUAGE?

Motivation

☐ Lowering the affective filter: Like Step 1, having students respond in a complete sentence when appropriate serves as a linguistic scaffold. Modeling is key here. If teachers can model exactly what a correct response in the target language should sound like, students will be more likely to respond with confidence.

☐ Establishing structure and expectations: Once it becomes a norm, students will be more comfortable and motivated to participate because it is part of the classroom culture.

☐ Enhancing students' ability to sound smarter: Don't underestimate the power of this, especially with secondary students! The ability to respond in this manner will make students feel that they sound smarter because they can give a complete answer in the target language.

Access to Language

☐ Experiencing exposure to various models of the target language: Students are not receiving input just from the teacher — they are receiving it from the other students, as well. As some students will naturally be further along in their second language acquisition journey, they can actually be sources of i+1, or that more sophisticated language that is slightly above a student's current linguistic ability or comprehension level.

☐ Receiving repeated exposure to multiple targeted structures: This strategy offers practice in the language development of vocabulary, grammar structures, pronunciation, proper questioning techniques, and conversation cues. The repetition of sentence stems seamlessly offers students language production (or output) practice. This gives them real exposure to the syntax of the target language and an understanding of how that translates into discourse. This will prepare them for increased accuracy and language control in their performance and proficiency in spoken and written language.

☐ Becoming familiar with authentic forms of the language: Even when we use social language, we generally talk in full sentences. We don't usually communicate in fragments. When a class establishes the habit of communicating in complete sentences, students receive a more natural and authentic form of speech patterns in the target language.

What does research show about the effectiveness of students speaking and writing in complete sentences as a means of increasing comprehension and language development?

By using complete sentences, students are both receiving input and producing output in the target language. As students receive more input in the context of a language-rich classroom with low-stress opportunities to produce output, this will strengthen their second language development (Krashen, 1982; Swain, 1995). Research indicates that in order for students to use language accurately in their speaking and writing, they must hear the language multiple times and in multiple contexts (NICHD, 2000). Having students speak in complete sentences provides a means for students to hear vocabulary used in context, not only by the teacher, but also by their peers. Michael Lewis' (1993) research on the lexical approach to second language teaching shows us that there is value in teaching students with lexis, or certain groups of words that make up fixed expressions in the target language. Lexis can be comprised of high-frequency sentence stems that are used to negotiate meaning or structure communication.

Teachers must remember that students cannot write in ways they do not speak. When students are proficient in oral language, they are more proficient in their reading and writing (Geva, 2006). The expectation and preparation of students to respond in complete sentences allows them to participate in learning in a formal way. Research on second language acquisition suggests the need to pay attention to both second language acquisition and language form (Schmidt, 2001). When students share and respond to the teacher and other students with complete sentences and specific grammatical structures, they are involved in a successful, integrated approach that will teach them form and meaning of the target language. Similarly, it facilitates the opportunity to assess both language and literacy development.

The research-based SIOP Model (Echevarria, Vogt, & Short, 2017) demonstrates that students need frequent opportunities for interaction in the ESL classroom in order to encourage elaborated responses to lesson concepts. This holds true for the foreign language classroom as well. A classroom culture that requires the use of complete sentences routinely fosters student elaboration, while a classroom using one-word responses to questions does not.

"When teacher initiations lead only to single-word or single-clause responses, there is little opportunity for the learners' language to be stretched, for students to focus on how they are saying something, or for giving them practice in using the language for themselves" (Gibbons, 2015, p. 32).

FAQ
FREQUENTLY ASKED QUESTIONS

San Juan, Puerto Rico

WHEN DO I INTRODUCE MY STUDENTS TO THIS NORM?

It's always best to introduce the practice of using complete sentences at the beginning of the school year (or semester, depending on how your students are scheduled for foreign language electives). Explain the expectation of accountable conversation with students first, and then explain how they are expected to participate in class discussions. Many teachers have found implementation easier than they thought once the goal and the expectations of the strategy were clearly communicated to students.

WILL IT STRAIN CLASSROOM CONVERSATION AND LIMIT STUDENTS' ABILITY TO EXPRESS THEMSELVES IF WE EXPECT THEM TO REPHRASE ANSWERS USING COMPLETE SENTENCES?

No. Rather than limiting classroom conversation, the expectation of using complete sentences in the classroom actually enhances the free flow of ideas. Elaboration is rare in classrooms where one-word and short phrase answers are the norm. In this situation, students do not hear other students regularly communicating with complete thoughts and sentences. Instead, they hear phrases and fragments in response to teacher questions. In contrast, when complete thoughts are the norm, students quickly become more comfortable elaborating and expressing their ideas. In the foreign language classroom, this will ignite a spark for them to look up new words and phrases to use as responses and in conversations. When students are asked open-

ended questions at a higher level, they are able to say much more by using complete sentences.

We do need to be careful, however, not to overdo the use of complete sentences in class. We do want students to respond in complete sentences when we ask them questions directly during whole-class interactions, but we do not expect them to communicate with complete sentences in every interaction. A simple guideline is to make sure that every time a new question or topic is introduced in a discussion, we reiterate the expectation for using complete sentences. If we are practicing having an open discussion, we can relax and allow the free flow of ideas. This also provides an opportunity to teach the use of fillers. Fillers are words or sounds that speakers use to indicate that they are not yet finished talking, but need a moment to think (i.e,. um, er, ah, you know). Providing fillers for student use will allow for authentic speech and a natural flow to the conversation among your students. It will also provide an insightful lesson in understanding native speech in the target language.

HOW DO I SUPPORT STUDENTS WHEN THEY STRUGGLE WITH THE USE OF COMPLETE SENTENCES?

In order to enable students to speak in complete sentences, sometimes we need to provide support that helps them be successful with this skill independently. Nancy Motley, author of Talk, Read, Talk, Write (2016), provides three steps to help when scaffolding complete sentences:

1. **Let students talk more!** If the only opportunity students are getting to practice the target language is the one or two times they are called on by the teacher, they are not receiving enough practice. Students need many opportunities for output throughout each lesson. Incorporating more partner talk and group collaboration will help increase each student's opportunity to speak.

2. **Tweak their talk.** Each time students are asked to share (turn and talk; think, pair, share; group discussion, etc.), the teacher should identify clear goals for student conversations in the target language. Some great phrases for this include: "I'm listening for…," "It should sound like…," or "Here's your sentence stem…"

3. **Coach for it!** Some students will need a lot of linguistic support, while others may only need a visual cue to remind them to form a complete sentence. When a student responds with one word or a short phrase, here are four strategies for "coaching" students to use complete sentences (ranging from most support to least support):

Choral Response: The teacher puts the student response in a complete sentence and asks the class to repeat it together.

Sentence Stem: The teacher provides the first half of the response, and the student repeats that part and completes the response.

Key Word or Phrase: The teacher provides a key word or phrase that the student should include in their response.

Gesture: The teacher provides a nonverbal gesture to cue the student to rephrase his or her response in a complete sentence (e.g., nodding while using both hands to demonstrate "stretching" an imaginary rubber band).

DO STUDENTS WITH DISABILITIES HAVE TO EXPRESS THEMSELVES USING COMPLETE SENTENCES TOO?

Yes! Unless a student has a disability with an Individualized Education Plan (IEP) that indicates otherwise, expect all students to participate. With a few simple techniques, everyone can be included in this process. Students learning a new language have to negotiate content and language structures simultaneously. Giving sentence starters in the target language like, "The answer is…" and "I think…" improves communication abilities for struggling learners. This technique eliminates juggling unfamiliar language structures, and it makes communication easier for students. Another strategy is to allow students to whisper answers that are repeated to the whole class. They will feel safe, supported, and involved.

SHOULD WE GIVE STUDENTS A SENTENCE STEM FOR EVERY KEY CONCEPT?

Sentence stems are perfect for introducing concepts and language structures and for assessing student understanding during a lesson. They provide the target language students need to communicate using new and unfamiliar terms. When sentence stems are used consistently in the classroom, students automatically start to respond in complete sentences without reminders. The habit of reframing the language of the question into a response is a skill that students internalize through multiple practice opportunities as well as teacher modeling.

The following sentence stems can be used in any classroom.

SUMMARIZING

I learned…

Today I understood…

I still don't understand…

The most important thing I learned today was …

Today we talked about…

SHARING

I feel…

In my opinion…

I predict that…

I agree/disagree that…

My view on this subject is ___ because…

JUSTIFYING

I think ___ because…

I agree/disagree with ___ because…

Another idea might be ___ because…

I was thinking that ___ should be…

ACCESSING PRIOR KNOWLEDGE

I already know …

__ reminds me of …

My experience with…

I would like to know more about…

I would compare ____ to ____ because…

Discussing ___ made me think about…

ELABORATING

___ is important because…

I chose ___ because…

The answer might also be ___ because…

I would agree or disagree with ____ because…

Another reason could be…

I would add ____ because…

SUMMARIZING

J'ai appris…

Aujourd'hui, j'ai compris…

Je ne comprends toujours pas…

La chose la plus importante que j'ai apprise aujourd'hui est…

Aujourd'hui, nous avons parlé de…

SHARING

J'ai l'impression que…

À mon avis…

Je prédis que…

Je suis d'accord / pas d'accord que…

Mon point de vue sur ce sujet est que ___ parce que…

JUSTIFYING

Je pense que ___ parce que…

Je suis d'accord / pas d'accord avec ___ parce que…

On pourrait aussi penser que ___ parce que…

Je pense que ___ devrait être…

ACCESSING PRIOR KNOWLEDGE

Je sais déjà que…

__ me fait penser à…

Mon expérience avec…

Je voudrais en savoir plus sur…

Je comparerais ____ avec ____ parce que…

Notre discussion sur ___ m'a fait penser à…

ELABORATING

____ est important parce que…

J'ai choisi ___ parce que…

La réponse pourrait aussi être ___ parce que…

Je serais d'accord / pas d'accord avec ___ parce que…

Une autre raison pourrait être que…

J'ajouterais que ____ parce que…

SUMMARIZING

Aprendí…

Hoy comprendí…

Todavía no comprendo…

Lo más importante que aprendí hoy fue…

Hoy hablamos sobre…

SHARING

Siento…

En mi opinión…

Predigo que…

Estoy de acuerdo/no estoy de acuerdo con que…

Sobre este tema opino que ___ porque…

JUSTIFYING

Creo que ___ porque…

Estoy de acuerdo/no estoy de acuerdo con ___ porque…

Otra idea podría ser ___ porque…

Estaba pensando que ___ debería ser…

ACCESSING PRIOR KNOWLEDGE

Ya sé…

__ me recuerda a …

Mi experiencia con…

Me gustaría saber más sobre…

Compararía ____ con ____ porque…

Hablar sobre ___ me hizo pensar en…

ELABORATING

___ es importante porque…

Elijo ___ porque…

La respuesta también podría ser ___ porque…

Estaría de acuerdo o no estaría de acuerdo con ____ porque…

Otro motivo podría ser…

Agregaría ____ porque…

SUMMARIZING

Ich habe gelernt…

Heute habe ich verstanden…

Ich verstehe noch nicht…

Die wichtigste Sache, die ich heute gelernt habe, ist…

Heute haben wir über … geredet.

SHARING

Ich meine…

Meiner Meinung nach…

Ich sage voraus,…

Ich stimme/ stimme nicht zu, dass…

Meine Meinung zu dem Thema ist ___, weil…

JUSTIFYING

Ich denke ___, weil…

Ich stimme ___ zu/nicht zu, weil…

Ein anderer Gedanke wäre ___, weil…

Ich denke, ___ sollte/n ___ sein.

ACCESSING PRIOR KNOWLEDGE

Ich weiß bereits …

__ erinnert mich an …

Meine Erfahrung mit…

Ich würde gern mehr über ___ wissen.

Ich würde ____ mit ____ vergleichen, weil…

Die Diskussion über ___ lässt mich über ___ nachdenken.

ELABORATING

____ ist wichtig, weil…

Ich habe ___ gewählt, weil…

Die Antwort könnte auch ___ sein, weil…

Ich stimme _____ zu oder nicht zu, weil…

Ein weiterer Grund könnte ___ sein.

Ich würde ____ hinzufügen, weil.

Step 2 ACTIVITIES

5. Daily Warm-Up

DESCRIPTION

The strongest way to begin each day in the LOTE classroom is with an engaging daily warm-up. Starting the class with a warm-up allows students to review and reflect on their learning from the previous day's lesson. It can also provide teachers with the opportunity to preview new vocabulary or language structures while accessing students' prior knowledge about a language concept.

DIRECTIONS

1. Have students create a designated spot in their interactive notebooks for a daily warm-up. You can also incorporate the use of a daily template (see example below).

2. Write a question or two (in the target language) on the board or on a slide that is reflective of the previous day's learning.

3. Provide sentence stems as scaffolds for each question, so students have a model of how to respond and what is expected of them.

4. You may allow students to use dictionaries, translators, or word walls to assist in completion.

5. This is also a great opportunity to ask more personal or reflective questions. Examples may include the following:

Yesterday I...	Hier, j'ai...
Something interesting that happened...	Il m'est arrivé quelque chose d'intéressant...
Let me tell you about...	Je voudrais vous parler de...
Today I will...	Aujourd'hui, je vais...
I hope...	J'espère...

Ayer yo...	Gestern, habe ich...
Sucedió algo interesante...	Etwas Interessantes, das passiert ist...
Déjame que te cuente sobre...	Lass/t mich über ... berichten.
Hoy...	Heute werde ich...
Espero...	Ich hoffe...

6. Sentence Stems for Starters *(Adapted from Escalante, 2018)*

DESCRIPTION
This is a fun and interactive activity to use after introducing students to the vocabulary used in describing common objects found in a backpack, purse, or wallet.

DIRECTIONS
1. Students may begin by writing the stems and answering the questions in their notebooks or journals.
2. You may allow students to use dictionaries, translators, or word walls to assist in utilizing new vocabulary or descriptions.
3. Have students share their stems with a shoulder partner.
4. Randomize and rotate around the room so students have opportunities to practice sharing the sentences with multiple partners.

SENTENCE STEMS:

- This is my _____. (license, water bottle, etc.)
- I keep ____ in my backpack/purse/wallet because _____.
- You might find it interesting that I _____.
- ____ from my backpack/purse/wallet indicates that I _____.
- My (backpack/purse/wallet) contains a _____ that I use when I _____.
- I find it convenient to have a _____ when I go ____.
- Based on the information found on/in my ___,

- C'est mon/ma _____. (permis, bouteille d'eau, etc.)
- Je mets ____ dans mon sac à dos / sac à main / portefeuille parce que _____.
- Il pourrait vous intéresser que je _____.
- ____ dans mon sac à dos / sac à main / portefeuille signifie que je _____.
- Mon/ma (sac à dos / sac à main / portefeuille) contient un _____ que j'utilise quand je _____.
- Je trouve pratique d'avoir un / une _____ quand je vais ____.
- En fonction des informations trouvées sur / dans mon ___,

- Esta es mi _____. (licencia, botella de agua, etc.)
- Tengo mi ____ en mi mochila/cartera/billetera porque _____.
- Quizás te parezca interesante que _____.
- ____ de mi mochila/cartera/billetera indica que _____.
- Mi (mochila/cartera/billetera) contiene un _____ que uso cuando _____.
- Me parece conveniente tener un _____ cuando voy a ____.
- En base a la información encontrada en mi ___,

- Das ist mein/e____. (Führerschein, Wasserflasche, etc.)
- Ich habe _____ in meinem/r Rucksack/Handtasche/Geldbörse, weil_____.
- Du findest vielleicht interessant, dass ich_____.
- ____ aus meinem/r Rucksack/Handtasche/Geldbörse, zeigt dass ich _____.
- In meinem/er (Rucksack/Handtasche/Geldbörse) befindet sich ein/e_____, die/den/das ich benutze, wenn ich _____.
- Ich finde es praktisch ein/e_____ zu haben, wenn ich _____ gehe.
- Laut der Informationen in/auf meinem/r _____,

Step 2 ACTIVIES

7. Ticket Out

DESCRIPTION

This quick and straightforward activity requires minimal preparation, but when implemented as a regular part of daily lessons, it has an incredible impact on the quality of written responses. "Ticket Out" asks students to write something about the linguistic or cultural focus of the day's lesson. This gives them immediate practice using target language that was just introduced. It also gives teachers an excellent way to check student understanding, and it provides tailor-made content for the next day's lesson.

DIRECTIONS

1. Ask students to reflect on what they learned at the end of the lesson or class period.

2. Have students write a "Ticket Out" using a sentence stem on a sticky note. A "Ticket Out" can be open-ended or very specific. Here are some examples:

I learned something new today, and it is... I think... What I learned today reminds me of... The term _____ means... I am still confused about... Tomorrow I hope to find out... The main idea of _____ is....	J'ai appris quelque chose de nouveau aujourd'hui, c'est que... Je pense... Ce que j'ai appris aujourd'hui me fait penser à... Le terme _____ signifie... Je ne comprends toujours pas très bien... Demain, j'espère apprendre... L'idée principale de _____ est...
Aprendí algo nuevo hoy y es... Creo... Lo que aprendí hoy me recuerda a... El término _____ significa... Todavía estoy confundido con... Espero mañana poder descubrir... La idea principal de _____ es...	Ich habe heute etwas Neues gelernt und zwar... Ich denke... Was ich heute gelernt habe erinnert mich an... Der Begriff_____ bedeutet... Ich verstehe .... noch nicht. Ich hoffe, dass ich morgen herausfinde... Der Hauptgedanke von _____ ist...

3. Collect the sticky notes and review them.

4. Use student responses to guide the next lesson.

5. Use an alternative "Ticket Out" approach. Have students record the sentence stems in their journals for future reference or for upcoming writing assignments.

8. Stem Wall

DESCRIPTION

Using a "stem wall" is similar to using a "word wall." Teachers post sentence stems in a highly accessible place for students to use throughout lessons.

DIRECTIONS

1. Identify stems that will be used throughout a unit or lesson.

2. List three to seven of those high-frequency stems in a clearly visible place with translations provided as necessary.

3. Model pronunciation of stems, and have students practice pronouncing the stems.

4. When participating in conversation or writing activities, direct students' attention to the stem wall, and set expectations regarding the use of the stems.

5. Ensure at least one of the listed stems will be used in a day's lesson by continually updating the list.

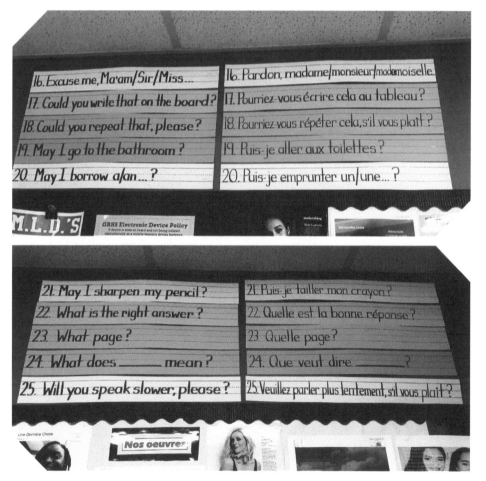

Photo courtesy of Lamar CISD

Step 2 ACTIVITIES

9. Slide Show

DESCRIPTION

Groups of students create "scenes" from a chosen topic or piece of text in the target language. Students prepare a series of scenes in small groups depicting a sequence of events (e.g., person traveling abroad, someone buying a home, etc.) or story line. The scenes are presented through *tableaux* (frozen scenes) where the students remain silent and motionless before changing to the next tableaux.

DIRECTIONS

1. Each group prepares a tableaux of frozen scenes using gestures. Facial expressions, body stance, positioning, and minimal props support each scene.

2. Have one or two students serve as narrators to describe the events or actions for the audience in the target language.

3. After watching each presentation, the class reads the passage or reviews the vocabulary from the topic that the group used for the slide show presentation.

4. Students may then discuss the various ways the group portrayed important ideas from the passage.

They demonstrated _____ by ...

They showed how ...

They represented the reasons why ...

I think they were trying to show ...

Ils ont prouvé _____ en...

Ils ont montré comment...

Ils ont décrit les raisons pour lesquelles...

Je pense qu'ils essayaient de montrer...

Lo demostraron _____ por...

Mostraron cómo...

Representaron los motivos por los que...

Creo que intentaban demostrar...

Sie zeigten _____ durch...

Sie zeigten wie...

Sie führten die Gründe auf, warum...

Ich denke, sie haben versucht zu zeigen...

(Adapted from Seidlitz & Perryman, 2011)

10. Roving Paragraph Frames *(Adapted from Salva & Matis, 2017)*

DESCRIPTION

Roving Paragraph Frames is an activity that combines listening, speaking, reading, and writing in an interactive format to benefit all learners. Students engage in a series of short conversations, each of which culminates in the creation of a new sentence in the target language. The collection of sentences eventually forms a paragraph. This strategy can be used as a warm-up activity, a transition midway through a class period, or as closure to review the day's concepts and learning.

DIRECTIONS

1. Give your students a sentence stem to begin the activity, and let them think and respond in writing with a complete sentence. Sample: *"When ordering in a cafe, it is important to_____."*

2. Ask the students to stand up with their paper and pencils when they have completed the written sentence.

3. Have the students "rove" around the room and find a partner.

4. Ask students to read their writing to one another in the target language. The first person reads his or her complete sentence (stem + response). The second person listens and then reads his or her own complete sentence.

5. The partners then collaborate to write a new sentence that begins with a new stem, such as *"In addition, _____."* They can either "borrow or steal" each other's responses if they were different, or they can create a fresh sentence.

6. Once sentence number two is complete, partners raise their hands or stand back to back. The key here is to incorporate total response signals to indicate to the teacher that the task is complete. Now they are ready to rove again!

7. Have the students find new partners, and repeat the entire process with the second partner. It is crucial to instruct students to take turns reading everything they have written so far and listening to each other's sentences. This validates student responses, and encourages the use of listening and speaking skills.

8. After reading individual sentences, students write a third sentence with the stem *"Also, _____."*

9. To conclude, have students repeat the process one last time, roving to find their final partners. Once each partner reads his or her individual sentences aloud, ask students to write the final sentence using the last stem *"Finally, _____."* At this point, each student should have a well-constructed paragraph in hand, complete with transitions and complete thoughts recorded in the target language.

• When ordering in a cafe, it is important to_____. • In addition, _____. • Also, _____. • Finally, _____.	• Lorsque vous commandez dans un café, il est important de_____ • De plus, _____. • Et aussi, _____. • Enfin, _____.	• Cuando pedimos algo en un café, es importante_____. • Además, _____. • También, _____. • Por último, _____.	• Beim Aufgeben einer Bestellung im Cafe, ist es wichtig_____. • Zusätzlich, _____. • Außerdem, _____. • Schließlich, _____.

STEP ③ *Randomize and Rotate When Calling on Students*

Photo courtesy of Anna Matis

Barcelona, Spain

What is Step 3?

Many teachers have struggled with finding ways to manage a classroom full of diverse learners with varying linguistic abilities and proficiencies. The same few students always raise their hands to respond as the rest of the class sits. We often end up calling on the energetic participators because they usually know the answer, and it allows us as teachers to maintain the pace of our lesson. Every so often we insist that other students respond, and we are met with frustration, anxiety, or blank stares.

SOLUTION 1: RANDOMIZING

Randomizing is one effective way to overcome this problem. It requires very little planning. We create a simple system, like using index cards or Popsicle™ sticks with each student's name, and we rely on that system when we call on students. This changes the way we ask questions. With rare exceptions, we avoid using phrases like these:

"Who can tell me…?"

"Let's see who knows…."

"Does anyone know …?"

"Can someone tell the class…?"

For the most part, these phrases encourage the participatory students who continue to shout out and dominate discussion. Our goal is to have everyone involved in discussions so that we can assess all students' understanding of concepts, not just those students who enjoy participating. More importantly, we want to provide entry points for target language practice to every student in the classroom. When we do not use random selection to assess students, we are only checking the understanding of a few highly motivated students. Moreover, only these students are receiving opportunities to practice language output. When randomizing, the questioning technique looks like this:

> Ask the question.
>
> Pause.
>
> Select a student to respond using a random selection system.

It is important to ask questions without the solicitation of volunteers. In some cases, it actually helps to explicitly ask students not to their raise hands; this eliminates the temptation to call only on those who volunteer. Pausing after the question gives everyone a chance to think, and it creates some positive tension as students wonder who will be chosen. Next, we use random selection by drawing an index card from a pile, for example. This ensures that all students are paying attention and have a fair chance to be called on to respond. Asking questions in this way promotes higher student engagement and more accurate assessment of student understanding. With this method, students grow accustomed to always being prepared to respond, and we grow accustomed to using cards, sticks, or even smartphone apps whenever we ask questions or have discussions.

SOLUTION 2: ROTATING

Using a rotation strategy, such as Spencer Kagan's Numbered Heads Together (Kagan & Kagan, 2009), is an easy way to get everyone involved and avoid the problems of calling on the same students again and again.

Here are the steps:

> Divide students into groups of four.

> Ask students to count off within the group (one through four) so each person has a number.

> Ask a question.

> Give groups a chance to talk to each other about the answer.

> Ask one number to stand up in each group. For example, "All threes, please stand."

> Have the number threes report for each group.

> Instruct students to respond with this sentence stem if they have the same response as another group: "We agree that _____ because..."

Repeat the procedure with other questions until each number from one through four has been called, giving every person an opportunity to speak for their group. This is a great opportunity for teachers to practice Total Physical Response (TPR) and assign gestures for standing up, etc., with physical commands in the target language. Numbered Heads Together is used best with open-ended questions that have more than one possible response. Of course, all students should share their answers in complete sentences.

Some other ways to randomize and rotate include marking a seating chart as students are called on, numbering desks, and using computer programs or smartphone apps to randomly select student names. In my classroom, I made color-coded index cards for each of my six class periods. The students completed these cards on the first day of school, with student and parent contact information on the front and responses to personal survey questions on the back. I would then use these cards not only for randomization, but also to call roll for daily attendance. After a few days, I handed this task off to my students! They would take turns pulling the correct class period's stack from the box at the front of the room, and one student per day would call roll by using students' self-selected French names. Not only would this save me time and effort, but students would get an additional opportunity to practice their French pronunciation and learn the French names of their fellow classmates almost seamlessly. Additionally, this was a highly motivating activity to get the students started each class period.

It is not important which system for randomizing and rotating we use, but it is important that we have a system in place. We must include everyone. Without a system, total participation is impossible.

There are times when it may be helpful to have an open dialogue without using index cards or seating charts. Similarly, teachers may like the energy of students calling out answers and freely exchanging ideas. These discussions can be positive experiences for some students, but they will rarely be positive for all students. If we do not have a system in place, we are leaving students out. Those students are usually at-risk pupils, students with special needs, or students who are disengaged, all of whom would most benefit from active participation.

TYPES OF RANDOMIZATION:
THE CHART BELOW PROVIDES SPECIFIC EXAMPLES OF DIFFERENT WAYS OF RANDOMIZING.

Characteristics Teacher randomizes based on student preferences/characteristics that students may share.	Birthdays, type of clothing, favorite sports teams, places to visit on vacation
Names in a 'Bank' Teacher writes student names on index cards, popsicle sticks, or uploads the names into smartphone apps for randomization.	Index cards, Popsicle® sticks, smartphone apps
Pairs/Groups Teacher uses these objects to randomize which partner or new group students will meet with next.	Playing cards, stickers on desks, matching pairs of cards (i.e. peanut butter and jelly, ketchup and mustard, etc.), appointment clocks, picture puzzles
Student Choices Teacher allows students to select the next person to respond based on various objects or characteristics.	**Beach ball:** Student tosses a ball, student who catches the ball answers **Volun-tell:** Student picks next person to respond (can be from the name bank) **Pick a Characteristic:** Student picks new characteristics (January birthdays, blue shirts, etc.)

Motivation

☐ **Encouraging accountability:** The process of randomization holds all students accountable for learning the content and preparing to respond, even when they are unsure of the answer. It goes hand in hand with Step 1 since the process has already taught students how to respond in the target language even when they're unsure!

☐ **Creating a game-like atmosphere:** The essence of this strategy is to infuse the class with a sense of positive tension and energy that is motivating and engaging as all students prepare to respond. Positive motivation can help lower the affective filter for reluctant students, as they know all other students in the class are being asked to perform the same task. Students know they can always use a Clarification Stem from Step 1 for assistance, additional information, or time to think. Additionally, Marzano's (2004) research shows that participating in "games" can reinforce deeper understanding of new vocabulary words or terms.

☐ **Establishing structure that creates equity and safety:** Step 3 is a classroom norm that is beneficial for motivation and even classroom management. When used correctly, students begin to see the use of randomization as a structure that establishes safety and equity because all students, regardless of their knowledge or ability, are held to the same expectations (Gewertz, 2005).

Access to Language

☐ **Reinforcing students' attention to comprehensible input:** When teachers randomize and rotate who is to be called on to respond, all students are forced to listen to and pay attention to input from the teacher. Without all students being asked to pay attention, there is no guarantee that all students will be listening for this input. If students don't receive comprehensible input with low-stress opportunities for output, there will be no language development.

☐ **Providing equitable access:** This step also ensures that all students have an opportunity to listen and learn. The teacher might not call on everyone, but everyone will have access to the input because everyone's name is on the class list, Popsicle® sticks, index cards, or randomizer app.

☐ **Encouraging the use of target language responses 100% of the time:** Randomization provides students with constant opportunities to practice responding in the target language. Even if they do not know the response (or were not paying attention), they always have an appropriate response if they use one of the Step 1 Clarification Stems in the target language, such as, "Could you please repeat the question?"

☐ **Providing opportunity to think in the target language:** Students have repeated opportunities to mentally practice the target language, even when they are not being called on. When students understand that they may be randomly selected to respond, they form their responses in their minds. The students can then check their mental responses by listening to the called-on student's oral response.

What additional research connects the use of randomization techniques to students' comprehension and language development?

Lee and VanPatten (2003) teach us that mastering a language occurs through substantial practice in highly engaging and low-stress environments. The goal of Step 3 is to create an environment where all students are engaged and encouraged to take part in responding — not only those whose hands are raised. Randomizing and rotating student responses is an important strategy to maintain a structure of accountability, especially during cooperative tasks (Johnson & Johnson, 1999). This practice supports all students by providing them with additional time to process information, and it gives teachers the opportunity to provide wait time after

questioning. Student engagement is also highly correlated to student achievement. In a study conducted by McDougall and Cordeiro (1993), students who attended lectures that utilized random questioning outperformed similar students by 20% in classes where random oral questioning was not used. The researchers suggest that random oral questioning increases student preparedness, attentiveness, and achievement. Schmoker (2006) and Bickel and Bickel (1986) state that it is not enough for teachers to focus on what is taught and how it is taught, but rather who is paying attention when it is taught. Learning increases when students are focused on tasks during instruction. Research shows that content-based tasks that help students notice, retrieve, and generate language are effective in facilitating second language acquisition (Long,1996, 2007).

Photo courtesy of Frisco ISD

FAQ

Labadee Island, Haiti

HOW OFTEN SHOULD WE USE RANDOMIZING AND ROTATING FOR QUESTIONING?

In order to check for student understanding, randomizing and rotating should take place in every classroom whenever there is whole-class discussion. Other kinds of questioning are effective for motivating students, getting new ideas on the table, creating resources, and generating creative energy. But if we want to check for understanding or create an inclusive environment, we must randomize or rotate whom we select to respond to questions.

It's not necessary to randomize every single question asked. A helpful guideline is to call on students randomly every time a new question, new language structure, or new topic is introduced. If students want to add thoughts or responses to an existing topic, it's all right for them to volunteer ideas. If we want to generate a flow of ideas on a topic after using random selection, we can open the class discussion to all.

WHAT SHOULD WE DO ABOUT STUDENTS WHO BLURT OUT ANSWERS?

Teaching students to refrain from blurting out answers is a skill that students can learn just like everything else they learn in school. A good starting point is to explain why we want students to avoid calling out answers. Setting up a role-play with two students having a conversation and a third student who constantly interrupts provides a clear example for students. After watching this role-play, ask students what they think of the interruptions, and have them write their responses. Most students will describe such behavior as rude, unkind, anti-social, immature, etc. Explain that when we call on a student by name, we have begun a conversation. If others choose to talk over the conversation, they are interrupting, and this behavior shows them in an unfavorable light.

Sometimes there is a difference between blurting out answers and speaking without raising a hand. With secondary students, it is unrealistic to tell students they can never talk without raising their hands. This is not the way academic discourse usually takes place among adults in professional and university settings. There are some types of discussions where raising hands or waiting for the speaker to call on someone inhibits the free flow of ideas. In order to maintain a respectful classroom culture, we want students to avoid calling out and interrupting others on these three occasions:

1. When we are using a randomizing system
2. When we call on another student by name
3. When another student has not finished expressing ideas

Most students see these guidelines as reasonable and agree that they build a safer classroom environment for students to answer questions and express views. Establishing these guidelines early in the year and enforcing them consistently is critical to their success.

SHOULD WE PLACE THE INDEX CARDS AND POPSICLE™ STICKS BACK IN THE STACK, OR SHOULD WE TAKE THEM OUT ONE BY ONE TO MAKE SURE EVERYONE GETS A CHANCE TO RESPOND?

Different teachers have different answers to this question. Some students know they will no longer be called upon when their stick or card is removed, and they check out of the discussion. This problem can be solved a few ways:

1. Return the cards to the bottom of the stack. Draw mostly from the top half of the stack, occasionally drawing from the bottom so that student names have the potential of occurring again.

FAQ CONTINUED

2. Use a set of "inside/outside cups" for the sticks. Let the "outside" cup that is larger in size hold the student names who have not yet been called, and let the smaller "inside" cup hold student names who have already been called. Draw from the outside cup during discussions, but occasionally draw from the inside cup so that names can be called again.

3. Combine randomizing and rotating. During a discussion using Numbered Heads Together, call on all the twos to share. Afterward, randomly call on a student to respond to what the two said by using the sentence starter, "I agree/disagree with 'Gunther' that…"

WHAT ABOUT STUDENTS WHO ARE WAY BEHIND THEIR PEERS? WON'T IT EMBARRASS THEM IF WE CALL ON THEM?

Teaching students what to say when they don't know the answer (Step 1, p. 40) solves this problem. Students can feel confident when called upon because, even if they do not have the answer, they always have an appropriate response in the target language, such as, "May I please have some more information?"

WILL IT DISCOURAGE STUDENTS WHO WANT TO SHARE IF I RANDOMIZE AND ROTATE RESPONSES? WILL THEY NOT WANT TO PARTICIPATE IF I REDIRECT THEM WHEN THEY BLURT OUT ANSWERS?

Students who like to talk and share in class are sometimes frustrated at first when they can no longer be the center of the teacher's attention. Many students are used to dominating classroom discussions, and their sense of self-worth is tied to their ability to answer questions and share thoughts. Sometimes

these students will complain about the use of randomization techniques. We can solve this by using Numbered Heads Together, varying our questioning techniques, and increasing the amount of student-to-student interaction.

Students learning to listen actively to one another is an additional benefit of randomizing and rotating student responses. Sometimes students who dominate discussions don't realize that other students who are quieter or less proficient may have great ideas to share. By giving students who are used to talking more of a chance to slow down and hear what other students have to say, they learn both patience and tolerance for another student's point-of-view. They also hear various models of the target language being spoken, which can actually scaffold a learner's increased understanding. The students who don't respond frequently in class or share in discussions learn that their views are valuable and that they can successfully contribute to a healthy exchange of ideas. These practices are essential if we hope to strengthen the skill of meaningfully participating in conversations in a new language.

Actively discussing these classroom behaviors and attitudes in class can be very beneficial for every student. Some students do not recognize that their behavior is hindering other learners. Open discussions regarding participation and engagement in academic settings can prepare students for healthier interactions in the future. This is a way of establishing not only rules of conduct but a classroom culture based on mutual respect. Research has shown that classroom management is facilitated when expectations for behavior and participation are explicitly stated and explained (Johnson, Stoner, & Green, 1996.)

11. Numbered Heads Together

DESCRIPTION

This rotation strategy enables all students, in small groups, to share with the whole class. It is an easy way to get everyone involved and avoid the problems of calling on the same students again and again. Numbered Heads Together is used best with open-ended questions that have more than one possible response. Of course, all students should share their answers in complete sentences. Some other ways to randomize and rotate include marking a seating chart as students are called on, numbering desks, and using computer programs to randomly select student names. The important thing is not which system we use, but that we have a system in place. It is important to include everyone. Without a system, total participation is impossible.

DIRECTIONS

1. Divide students into groups of four.
2. Ask students to count off within the group (one through four) so each person has a number.
3. Ask a question.
4. Give groups a chance to talk to each other about the answer.
5. Ask one number to stand up in each group. For example, "All ones, please stand."
6. Have the number one students report for each group.
7. Instruct students to respond with this sentence stem if they have the same response as another group: "We agree that _____ because…"
8. Repeat the procedure with other questions until each number from one through four has been called, giving every person an opportunity to speak for their group. The teacher can also randomize which number will speak in which order.

All Ones, please stand.	Tous les Uns, levez-vous. .
We agree that _____ because...	Nous sommes d'accord que _____ parce que...
Todos los Unos, párense.	Steht bitte alle zusammen auf.
Estamos de acuerdo con que _____ porque...	Wir stimmen zu, dass_____ weil...

(Adapted from Kagan & Kagan, 2009)

FOREIGN LANGUAGE CLASSROOM   81

Step 3 ACTIVITIES

12. Picture Puzzles

DESCRIPTION

Picture Puzzles is a cooperative learning activity in which student groups are formed by mixing and matching "puzzle pieces" of images together. You may, of course, use actual puzzle pieces if you have them! If not, pictures from the Internet or magazines can serve this purpose.

DIRECTIONS

1. Before class, the teacher selects images on paper to cut into enough "puzzle pieces" so each student in class will receive a piece. Pictures can be representative of the target language and culture or more specific to the current unit of study.

2. Teachers will need as many whole "puzzles" or pictures as small groups. If the idea is to have six small groups, then six images need to be used.

3. When students walk into class that day, they are each either given or asked to randomly select one puzzle piece. They will use this piece to form groups later on.

4. After receiving whole-group instruction from the teacher or reading informative text, students move to find their corresponding puzzle pieces (the new small groups).

5. Small groups can then participate in various group activities, such as answering discussion questions together, having structured conversations regarding the text, or creating an anchor chart to demonstrate their learning.

6. Alternatively, the learning activity can be jigsawed so each student on a team is assigned a piece of a text to read or a part of a topic to investigate. Students complete their sections independently then come back together as a group and share their sections or help assemble a team product by contributing a piece of the "puzzle."

13. Appointment Clocks

DESCRIPTION

This is a quick and easy way to get students into pairs. It is especially helpful for structuring student conversations with varying speaking partners so students have practice with different classmates and can hear different models of the target language.

DIRECTIONS

1. Each student is given a clock face with blanks at each hour.

2. Students make appointments with each other and pair up accordingly anytime during the lesson when students need to work in pairs. Teachers may choose to only have students find partners at the 3:00, 6:00, 9:00, and 12:00 time slots, or they may have one partner per "hour."

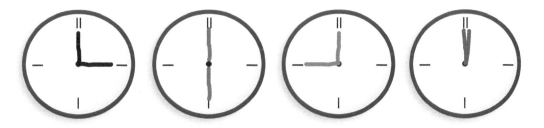

Students please meet with your 6:00 partner to share...	Classe, partagez avec votre partenaire en face (à votre 6h00)...
Estudiantes reúnanse con su compañero ubicado a las 6:00 para compartir...	Bitte trefft euch mit eurem 6:00 Uhr Partner, um über... zu reden.

Step 3 ACTIVITIES

14. Travel Buddies

DESCRIPTION

Much like Appointment Clocks, the purpose of Travel Buddies is to give students the opportunity to pair up with various classmates in a foreign language classroom. Partnering with different students for structured conversations and speaking activities gives students the opportunity to negotiate meaning from a variety of "sources" of language input.

DIRECTIONS

1. Each student is given a map of the world with blank spaces under the continents instead of the names.

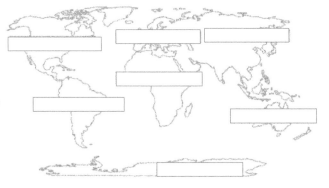

2. Students walk around the room and find "buddies" to travel with to each of the continents. Students can only pair with a particular student one time while they complete the map. They will have seven total speaking partners.

3. Students locate and pair up with their travel buddy from a certain country of the teacher's choosing at anytime during the lesson when students need to work in pairs.

> Students please meet with your partner from South America to share...

> Classe, partagez avec votre partenaire d'Amérique du Sud...

> Estudiantes reúnanse con su compañero de América del Sur para compartir...

> Trefft euch bitte mit eurem Partner aus Südamerika, um über .... zu reden.

(Adapted from Yzquierdo, 2017)

15. Inside/Outside Cups

DESCRIPTION

The purpose of using Inside/Outside Cups when calling on students is to prevent the same students from always being called. Students names are placed on Popsicle™ sticks inside of a plastic cup for randomization. However, some students know they will no longer be called upon when their stick is removed, and they check out of the discussion. This problem can be solved using the method outlined below.

DIRECTIONS

1. Use a plastic cup to hold the classroom set of popsicle sticks. Locate two cups of varying sizes, so a smaller cup can easily fit inside the larger one.

2. Randomly select a student's name from the cup when asking a question. Let the "outside" cup that is larger in size hold the names that have not yet been called, and let the smaller "inside" cup hold names that have already been called.

3. Draw from the outside cup during discussions; occasionally draw from the inside cup so that names can be called again.

4. A helpful guideline is to call on students randomly every time a new question, new language structure, or a new topic is introduced.

(Adapted from Seidlitz & Perryman, 2011)

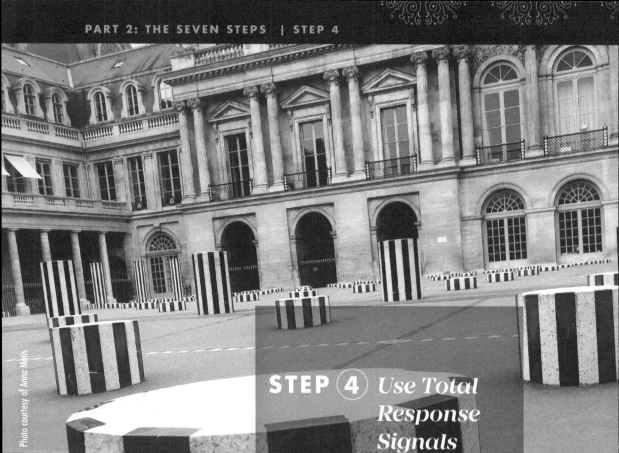

Photo courtesy of Anna Matis

STEP ④ Use Total Response Signals

Paris, France

What is Step 4?

Total response signals are cues students can use to indicate they are ready to respond to a question or ready to move on to new material. Response signals allow students to prepare for oral or written participation in a nonthreatening way, and they provide the teacher a very effective tool for gauging student understanding in real time.

There are three elements of an effective total response signal:

TOTAL: Total response signals include every student in the classroom: at-risk students, ELLs, students with special needs, gifted students, oppositional and defiant students, and students with interrupted formal education. Total means everyone.

RESPONSE: Every student will respond. After questions are posed, students are given an opportunity to make a decision. Students think through what they know to decide how to respond.

SIGNAL: Once students have responded or made decisions, they will indicate their responses with a visible signal. The signal must be clear enough so that we can immediately survey how many students can respond to the question or make a decision.

Here's how it might sound in a foreign language classroom. The dialogue would take place in the target language:

TEACHER Okay, everyone, take a look at the restaurant menu on your desks. Show me thumbs-up as soon as you can find the entrées. *(Students begin to put their thumbs up as they find the entrée section on their menus. The teacher notices a few students struggling, walks to their desks, and points out the location of the entrées with her finger. These students then put their thumbs up.)*

Okay, I see everyone has found the entrées. Now, I'm going to give you a sentence starter. I'm going to select someone to finish this sentence: "The first item in the entrée section of the restaurant menu is…." *(Teacher selects Popsicle™ stick from bucket.)* Lyn?

LYN The first item in the entrée section of the restaurant menu is steak au poivre.

TEACHER Thank you, Lyn. Now, everyone find the desserts on the restaurant menu. Show me a thumbs-up when you can find it…

Total response signals enable us to consistently check for student understanding. We think of them as instant, ongoing assessments used throughout a lesson. With response signals, we don't have to wait for the quiz, test, worksheet, or writing assignment to find out how well our students understand a topic. We can immediately check for understanding and see who is ready to move on and who still needs help. There are four basic types of response signals:

WRITTEN RESPONSE Students write their responses on paper, sticky notes, cards, white boards, or chalk boards and hold them up so they are visible to the teacher.

READY RESPONSE Students show they have finished a task or are ready to begin a new task. For example, the "thinker's chin" means that students keep their fists on their chins until they finish thinking and are ready to respond to a question. When they are ready, they remove their fists from their chins.

MAKING CHOICES Students show their response to a given set of choices using a physical object or signal. For example, give students letter cards, labeled A, B, C, and D when reviewing a multiple choice test. After reading a question, ask students to show their choices. We can instantly see how students respond to each question. You can also premake True/False or Yes/No cards for students to use in response to many activities in the classroom.

RANKING Students show their relative degree of agreement or disagreement with particular statements. For example, ask students if they agree or disagree with the following statement: "We should visit Heidelberg instead of Berlin." Have students show their degree of agreement or disagreement using the following scale: five fingers to signal strong agreement, four fingers to signal agreement, three fingers to signal neutrality, two fingers to signal disagreement, and one finger to signal strong disagreement. Students should be ready to explain their reasoning.

1 - no clue
5 - I can teach it to
someone

The chart below gives specific examples of each type of response signal.

WRITTEN RESPONSE	• Hold up paper • Whiteboard • Personal chalkboards • Responses on cards
READY RESPONSE	• Hands up when ready • Hands down when ready • Thinker's chin (hand off chin when ready) • Stand when you are ready • Sit when you are ready • Put your pen on your paper when you are ready • Put your pen down when you are ready • All eyes on teacher • Heads down
MAKING CHOICES	• Open hand/closed hand • Thumbs up/thumbs down • Pens up/pens down • Number wheels • Green card/red card • Move to the corner/spot you agree/disagree with • Letter or number card choices on a metal ring – ABCD or 1234
RANKING	• Rank with your fingers • Rank with your arm (the higher, the better) • Line up according to reponse • Knocking/Clapping/Cheering

Photo courtesy of Lamar CISD

Motivation

☐ Providing opportunity for student choice: Teachers can see — and students can experience — gains in achievement when student choice is allowed in the selection of activities, texts, or products. It works the same way with response signals.

☐ Enabling students to self-assess and notice their own accomplishments: Students have a sense of control over their learning and comprehension when they're asked to self-assess and truly reflect on their learning and comprehension. The sense of accomplishment can be a great motivator when students are able to show that they truly understand the new material in the target language.

☐ Promoting positive tension and a game-like atmosphere: Much like in Step 3, the selection of signals coupled with physical movement can ignite a spark in students' energy that promotes the same sense of positive tension and game-like atmosphere that is fostered when we randomize and rotate our calling on students.

☐ Improving student-teacher relationships: Because the student sees the teacher adjusting the rate of instruction according to students' proficiency and needs, students can become more motivated to participate if they see that someone cares about the fact that they are learning.

Access to Language

☐ Enabling the teacher to adjust input to students' proficiency levels throughout the lesson: This step ensures that students receive instruction that is tailored to their needs. Whether that means repeating a question or concept in the target language at a slower pace or scaffolding the language with additional comprehensible input, students can receive greater access to language.

☐ Providing opportunities for peer-to-peer clarification: When used as a tool for formative assessment, total response signals allow students to see whether or not other classmates share the same level of understanding. Teachers can then use this knowledge and have students turn to each other to clarify meaning.

☐ Offering low-stress opportunities for output: When the total response signal being used is one that asks students to provide a quick written response, this is a great opportunity for low-stress output. Students who may be unsure of an answer or hesitant to respond out loud can write their responses for initial self-assessment.

☐ Allowing time for thinking and lowering the affective filter: Total response signals are sometimes called "ready responses" because they are used to indicate student readiness when it becomes time to respond to a question or command. These signals allow us to lower the affective filter in the classroom by only calling on students when we know they are prepared.

What is the research that shows the effect of total response signals on students' comprehension and language development?

Using active response signals has a positive effect on student achievement when compared with passive responses (Knapp & Desroachers, 2009). Research demonstrates that student engagement increases attention, which increases student achievement (Jensen, 2005). Active response signals are a powerful way to get students' attention because they connect physical movement with mental processes. Researchers also agree that active learning produces the greatest success (Echevarria & Graves, 2015). Total response signals facilitate the informal assessment of students' academic- and language-skill development throughout the lesson.

"It doesn't really matter which strategy you use as long as you include the learners in the decision. Offering students choices in how they learn gives them insight into their own metacognition as well as helping them become their own learning advocates. A side effect of relinquishing some pedagogical control is that the classroom becomes a warmer, more joyful place. You are demonstrating your compassion for them by allowing them to select their options" (Wilson, 2016).

San Miguel de Allende, Mexico

CHANEL   CHANEL   CHANEL   CHANEL

Paris, France

HOW DO YOU MAKE SURE STUDENTS USE RESPONSE SIGNALS CORRECTLY? WON'T MANY OF THEM SHOW A SIGNAL EVEN THOUGH THEY'RE NOT READY JUST BECAUSE ALL THE OTHER STUDENTS ARE SHOWING A SIGNAL?

This can be a problem if we aren't intentional about how to use total response signals. It is crucial to structure the use of response signals so that students are relaxed and honest when they use them. We also have to be respectful and encouraging when students do not show us a signal. If we ask students to raise their hands when they are ready to respond and many students are still sitting with their hands down, we have to be supportive and assume they would raise their hands if they had a response. At this point, we can rephrase the question, or ask everyone to put their hands down, clarify the information, and then ask the question again.

Providing variety for students to respond after a response signal helps students participate authentically. Sometimes students can share their thoughts with each other; other times we randomly select a student who will share with the class. If we always have students share with each other after giving us a response signal, many will show signals even though they are not ready to respond because they know they can rely on their partners for ideas. Randomizing after a response signal reduces this tendency.

Here is an example of what holding students accountable for use of total response signals might sound like in a more advanced foreign language classroom. The dialogue would take place in the target language:

TEACHER Okay, what do you think was the motive for Turkish immigrants leaving their home country? Raise your hand as soon as you have thought about a reason for the Turkish immigrants leaving and settling in Germany. *(All students raise their hands. Teacher randomly selects Giovanni's name from stack of cards.)* Giovanni, what do you think?

GIOVANNI May I please have some more information?

TEACHER Maybe I wasn't clear. Let me try again. Okay class, raise your hand as soon as you have an answer. Please don't raise your hand until you are ready to respond. That way I can make sure everybody's ready before I make a choice. *(Most students raise their hands. Some are still not raised.)*

TEACHER Okay, let's talk again about motive. Motive is the reason you do something. Think about what we read yesterday. Remember when Mehmet left home? Mehmet was a Turkish immigrant. Why do you think he left? Raise your hand when you can finish this sentence: Mehmet's motive for leaving Turkey was… *(All students raise their hands.)* Giovanni, what do you think?

GIOVANNI Mehmet's motive for leaving was because his family was looking for better job opportunities.

FAQ CONTINUED

WHAT IF STUDENTS STILL WON'T SHOW A RESPONSE SIGNAL EVEN AFTER AMPLE TIME IS GIVEN?

If students won't show a response signal after ample time has been given, the first step is to ask everyone to put their hands down or stop showing a signal. Then slowly repeat the concept, question, or instructions. Next, ask if anyone needs help understanding, and give students a chance to clarify misunderstandings with someone sitting near them. Then repeat your request for students to give a response signal. If there are still a few students who don't understand, we might work with them individually or ask if they understand what they are being instructed to do.

Sometimes it is possible to think decisions and tasks are easier than they are for our students. If more than two students delay too long in showing a response signal, we need to think about how well students really understand the task or the concept. The whole purpose of a response signal is to assess student understanding. If students are telling us they don't understand, then the signals are working well. A lack of response signals tells us where we need to reteach and refocus our instruction.

WON'T STUDENTS JUST LOOK TO SEE WHAT OTHER STUDENTS' SIGNALS ARE AND THEN COPY THOSE RESPONSES?

Yes, many students will do that. However, there are some strategies that can be used to overcome this problem. One strategy to eliminate mimicking when using letter cards is to print the letters on one side only; another is to have students sit in rows or at tables in positions where they cannot easily see how other students are responding. An alternative is to ask students to show their choices on a count of three or when we say, "Go." When students realize the signals are used to help support them when they don't understand and to find out what they think about various ideas, it is more likely they will show their honest understanding and choices with the signals.

WHAT ABOUT STUDENTS WITH SPECIAL NEEDS WHO CAN'T USE CERTAIN SIGNALS?

We need to be sensitive to what our students are physically capable of doing, and we have to avoid putting students in awkward situations by choosing to use total response signals. If a student has limited mobility and the response signal involves moving around the room, we want to make sure to give that student other options to express choice. If a student's level of cognitive development limits understanding or choices, modify or clarify the question in such a way that special-needs students can participate in the conversation meaningfully.

For the AP® Foreign Language Course Instructor and the IB Diploma Programme Language Acquisition Instructor

Steps 3 and 4 are essential to success for each student in your course. They allow you to select students in a neutral manner and to provide them with opportunities to show their proficiency in the target language. The curricular requirements of an AP® course suggest this as a mandate for teachers. It is stated that "the course provides opportunities for students to demonstrate (1) their proficiency in spoken and written interpersonal communication, (2) their ability in interpretive communication to understand and synthesize information, and (3) their proficiency in spoken and written presentational communication" (College Board, n.d., p.36). Using these techniques will allow you to have a more egalitarian classroom where every student has the opportunity to show their proficiency in the target language.

Photo courtesy of Lamar CISD

Step 4 ACTIVITIES

16. Total Response Signals

DESCRIPTION

Total Response Signals are a way for teachers to enable students to self-assess and refocus during classroom instruction. Through this method, students can instantly show their current level of understanding or their thoughts on a particular issue or question without impeding the flow of instruction. This activity is particularly effective when working with those in the beginning stages of second language acquisition, who may not be quite comfortable with verbal output.

DIRECTIONS

1. Ask the students a question.

2. Tell all the students to show you a nonverbal signal that will indicate the choice they have made. (See chart on page 88.)

3. Make sure all students have indicated a response. This is the most significant step of Total Response Signals. Responding to the students when only high achievers have answered defeats the purpose of a total response signal.

4. After all students have indicated their response, have students share their thoughts with one another. Provide sentence stems to scaffold the language.

5. Once students are more comfortable speaking, you might consider adding a last step in which you randomly select a student to share his or her thoughts with the whole class.

(Adapted from Seidlitz & Perryman, 2011)

17. Number Wheel Conversation

DESCRIPTION

This is a strategy to help students at higher levels of proficiency engage in conversation on a particular topic. Students rate their agreement or disagreement with statements or ideas and then discuss their thoughts with peers and the class.

DIRECTIONS

1. Set up: Provide students with a number ring. A number ring is made of index cards on a binder ring with the numbers one through five listed on one side of the cards, and the letters A through E listed on the other side.

2. Present students with a statement or question, and ask that they respond using their number ring. The lettered side works best with questions that have multiple choice answers. The number range works best with questions or statements requiring answers based on a gradation scale.

Which European country would you want to live in? A. United Kingdom B. Germany C. France D. Spain E. Italy	Dans quel pays européen aimeriez-vous habiter? A. Royaume-Uni B. Allemagne C. France D. Espagne E. Italie	¿En qué país de Europa te gustaría vivir? A. Reino Unido B. Alemania C. Francia D. España E. Italia	In welchem europäischen Land würdest du gern leben? A. Großbritannien B. Deutschland C. Frankreich D. Spanien E. Italien
On a scale of 1 to 5 how strongly do you agree or disagree?	Sur une échelle de 1 à 5, dans quelle mesure êtes-vous d'accord ou pas d'accord?	En una escala del 1 al 5, ¿qué tanto estás de acuerdo o en desacuerdo?	Wie stark stimmst du auf einer Skala von 1 bis 5 zu oder nicht zu?

Have students write down reasons for their selection in the target language.

3. Pair students up with students who selected the same letter or number, and have the pairs discuss reasons for their selection using the perspective and discussion stems in the target language (see pgs. 66-67). Students can add any of their partners' ideas to their list if they wish.

4. Now pair students with students who selected a different letter or number, and have them discuss the reasons for their selection using the perspective and discussion stems in the target language.

OPTIONAL → *Have students write a paragraph justifying their point of view*

Step 4 ACTIVITIES

18. Simon Says

DESCRIPTION

Simon Says is the classic game that teachers have used over the years to teach students commands, along with the importance of attentive listening. In the foreign language classroom, this game is especially effective for teaching verbs, nouns, and even adjectives. It also provides students the opportunity to practice imperative forms in the target language.

Simon Says has various names in other languages, some of the most common being "Jacques a dit" in French, "Simón dice" in Spanish, and "Kommando Pimperle" (or, with similar rules, "Alle Vögel fliegen hoch") in German.

DIRECTIONS

1. Decide if the game should be played whole class or with teams. It might be best to model first as a whole group and then divide the class into two teams. If the team approach is selected, one student from each team is asked to stand or sent to the front of the classroom.

2. The teacher, as Simon, shouts commands in the target language for students to "stand up," "sit down," "raise your hand," etc. These commands must be preceded by "Simon says" in the target language. For example, "Simon says raise your hand."

3. Students obey the command unless the teacher does not say "Simon says" before the command. Students are out, or must sit down, if they perform a command when the teacher did not say "Simon says."

4. Keep playing this game until all students are out. If playing in teams, each set of students per round must get three commands correct to receive a point.

5. Use this as an opportunity to practice vocabulary for body parts as well as target language verbs for basic classroom gestures and commands. You can capitalize on this later by utilizing these commands when teaching with student response signals.

6. For added language practice, allow students to become "Simon" and give commands to classmates.

SIMON SAYS	JACQUES A DIT	SIMÓN DICE	SIMON SAGT
stand up	levez-vous	pararse	Steht auf
sit down	asseyez-vous	sentarse	Setzt euch
raise your hand	levez la main	levantar la mano	Hebe deine Hand
Simon says raise your hand	Jacques a dit levez la main	Simón dice levanten la mano	Simon sagt, hebe deine Hand

19. Value Line

DESCRIPTION
The value line provides an opportunity for students to practice the target language by choosing and defending a position on an issue.

DIRECTIONS
Set up: Post the numbers one through five on separate papers, in a line, across a wall.

1. Write a statement about an issue that you think the students will have varying degrees of agreement on.

2. Tell the students to rate their agreement or disagreement with the statement using the following scale:

1 - Strongly Disagree 2 - Disagree 3 - Neutral 4 - Agree 5 - Strongly Agree I selected ___ because... I feel... In my opinion... I agree/disagree that... My view on this subject is ___ because...	1 - Pas du tout d'accord 2 - Pas d'accord 3 - Neutre 4 - D'accord 5 - Tout à fait d'accord J'ai choisi ___ parce que... J'ai l'impression que... À mon avis... Je suis d'accord / pas d'accord que... Mon point de vue sur ce sujet est que ___ parce que...	1 - Totalmente en desacuerdo 2 - En desacuerdo 3 - Neutro 4 - De acuerdo 5 - Totalmente de acuerdo Elegí ___ porque. . . Siento... En mi opinión... Estoy de acuerdo/no estoy de acuerdo con que... Sobre este tema opino que ___ porque...	1- stimme überhaupt nicht zu 2 - stimme nicht zu 3 - neutral 4 - stimme zu 5 - stimme stark zu Ich habe ___ gewählt, weil... Ich fühle... Meiner Meinung nach... Ich stimme/ stimme nicht zu, dass... Meine Meinung zu dem Thema ist ___, weil...

3. Have students write their level of agreement/disagreement on an index card.

4. Tell students to walk to and stand under the number on the wall that matches their index card.

5. Have students participate in a series of conversations in the target language. First, with others who either picked the same number or a "neighboring" number. Then with students who chose a position at least two numbers away.

6. Have students write short paragraphs (two to five sentences) defending their point of view.

(Adapted from Kagan & Kagan, 2009)

Step 4 ACTIVITIES

20. Green Card, Yellow Card, Red Card

DESCRIPTION

Green Card, Yellow Card, Red Card is a type of response signal system that allows teachers to regularly check in with students in various situations.

DIRECTIONS

1. Provide each student with a set of three cards (one green, one yellow, one red), and have the cards available at their desks or in their folders.

2. Explain to the students that they will use the cards as responses so that you can quickly ascertain their level of agreement, understanding, or confidence during class activities.

   a. **Level of Agreement:** Make a statement, and ask the students if they *agree* (green), *disagree* (red), or are *neutral* (yellow).

   b. **Check for Understanding:** At any point during a lesson ask students how well they are understanding. *I understand* (green) *I understand, but need you to slow down* (yellow). *I don't understand* (red).

   c. **Level of Confidence:** After an activity, ask students how confident they felt in their ability to participate in that activity. *I felt very confident* (green). *I felt somewhat confident* (yellow). *I didn't feel confident* (red).

(Adapted from Kagan & Kagan, 2009)

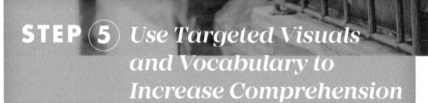

STEP ⑤ Use Targeted Visuals and Vocabulary to Increase Comprehension

Austrian window boxes

What is Step 5?

Step 5 involves being intentional about increasing student understanding of a target language through the use of visuals and vocabulary strategies. Targeted visuals are specific images, gestures, and objects that are used to increase comprehension in a target language. Teachers may or may not realize that basic instructional practices already in their repertoire contribute to making input comprehensible. For example, if a teacher is lecturing to students and gestures for students to stand up while asking them to stand up, that is a targeted visual. It is essential to fuse the use of visuals into all classroom instruction in the target language. Incorporating visuals in our lessons dramatically increases students' ability to understand and acquire target language lessons and concepts. It has been said that "a picture is worth a thousand words," and often this is true. Photos, maps, drawings, movie clips, and concrete objects give students access to vocabulary and language structures in spite of possible barriers such as lack of experience in the new language.

A key principle to keep in mind when trying to consistently use visuals is Point and Talk. This refers to the practice of continually referencing objects, images, and gestures whenever providing input in the new language. Point and Talk involves teachers intentionally developing the habit of thinking through what visuals and gestures they plan to use and how they will refer to them in each lesson. Teachers utilize these gestures to reference printed or posted language, visuals, and resources while giving directions to students and discussing content. This enables students to acquire vocabulary through context clues that boost comprehension. Even while giving directions, it is important to make eye contact with students and occasionally use response signals to measure student understanding of the content and directions. For example, you can tell your students, "Rate yourself on a scale of one to five with your hand showing how well you comprehend." You can read more about response signals on pg. 86.

The method of Total Physical Response (TPR) is along similar lines. TPR is a language acquisition method developed by James Asher (1969) that focuses on connecting physical movement with new language, especially in the form of commands. It is an approach that emphasizes providing comprehensible input in a very low-stress environment. TPR is often used for successfully teaching new vocabulary and grammar, such as active verbs.

Building on an initial understanding of TPR and the importance of gestures, Teaching Proficiency through Reading and Storytelling (TPRS) emerged in 1987. TPRS is a language acquisition approach developed by Blaine Ray that emphasizes providing large amounts of comprehensible input. This method centers on having students co-create stories with a teacher using targeted language structures (see TPRS pg. 111). Students then read texts that use the structures present in the co-created stories. In addition, TPRS classrooms emphasize providing opportunities for students to engage in reading texts in the target language, even at the beginning level. Three keys to developing fluency with TPRS are to ensure that the stories are comprehensible, repetitive (to enable practice of target language structures), and interesting.

Other strategies also help students acquire vocabulary in context. For example, Scanning is an activity that helps students acquire vocabulary whenever they read new material with unfamiliar words. To eliminate stumbling over these new words, we have students use scanning before a reading exercise begins. It doesn't take very much time for them to get used to this procedure, and it quickly builds students' understanding of new vocabulary. Scanning gives students some control over the vocabulary we emphasize, and it gives us the chance to focus on learning what they don't know instead of re-emphasizing what they already do know.

Scanning is a powerful, quick, and efficient tool used to build target language vocabulary skills for students. This strategy teaches students essential words for understanding new content minutes before they encounter the words in a text. Pre-teaching vocabulary with strategies such as scanning has led to significant gains in student achievement.

Here's how scanning works:

> The students survey a text. Beginners may start at the beginning of the document, trying to make sense of the text, noting words they simply can't make out. More advanced students should start at the bottom of a page and work up.
>
> The teacher generates a list of three to ten unfamiliar terms based on the students' survey.
>
> The teacher writes short, student-friendly definitions for the terms, giving definitions that match the way the word is used in the context of the passage.
>
> The students practice pronouncing the words during a choral reading with the teacher.
>
> The students read the passage.
>
> The students use some of the words during the speaking and writing tasks in the lesson. For example, students might scan words as they discuss the text with a partner, or they can use them in a written summary of the text.

Here's an example of what scanning might sound like in a typical classroom. Please note this first dialogue only serves as a translation. It is comprehensible only when the "scanned" vocabulary terms are imagined in the target foreign language, not in English. ⟶

TEACHER *(provides students with a piece of text about the humanitarian crisis in Venezuela)* Okay everyone, look at the text, and let's do a quick scan of unfamiliar words. Start at the bottom, scan toward the top, and circle two or more terms that you cannot define.

(Students begin circling words on their handouts.)

TEACHER Okay, I can see most of you have found a few words. Alessandra, tell me one of the words you selected.

ALESSANDRA "Scarcity."

TEACHER *(pauses and glances at poster)* Please express your thoughts in complete sentences.

ALESSANDRA I selected the word "scarcity."

TEACHER *(writes down "scarcity" on dry erase board)* Thanks. Julia, what was one of the words you selected?

JULIA I selected the word "average."

TEACHER *(writes down the word "average" on dry erase board)* Okay, does anyone else have a word that we should include? Leo?

LEO I'm not sure what "deteriorate" is, but I know we talked about it.

TEACHER Let's write that down too. *(writes "deteriorate" on the board)* Any other words?

BRUNO "Collapse."

TEACHER Okay these are great words. Does anyone know what "scarcity" means? Show me on a scale of one to five how much you agree with this statement: I know what scarcity means *(waits for student response)*. Okay, Leo, you showed a five. Can you tell me what scarcity means?

LEO Scarcity means "scarcity" in English.

TEACHER Very good! Does anyone know what "average" means? Show me on a scale of one to five how much you agree with this statement: I know what average means *(waits for student responses)*. Yes, Ted?

TED Isn't it "average" in English?

TEACHER Yes Ted, average is "average" in English.

TEACHER *(provides students with a piece of text about the humanitarian crisis in Venezuela)* Allez tout le monde, jetez un coup d'œil au texte et identifions les mots inconnus. Commencez par le bas du texte, parcourez-le en remontant et entourez au moins deux termes que vous ne comprenez pas.

(Students begin circling words on their handouts.)

TEACHER D'accord, je vois que la plupart d'entre vous ont identifié des mots. Alessandra, donne-moi l'un des mots que tu as choisis.

ALESSANDRA "La rareté."

TEACHER *(pauses and glances at poster)* Pourrais-tu formuler une phrase complète?

ALESSANDRA J'ai entouré le mot "la rareté."

TEACHER *(writes down "la rareté" on dry erase board)* Merci. Julia, peux-tu citer un des mots que tu as entourés?

JULIA J'ai entouré le mot "la moyenne."

TEACHER *(writes down the word "la moyenne" on dry erase board)* D'accord, quelqu'un a-t-il un mot à ajouter? Léo?

LEO Je ne suis pas sûr de la signification de "détériorer" mais je sais que nous en avons déjà parlé.

TEACHER *(writes "détériorer" on the board)* Alors notons-le aussi. Vous avez encore un mot?

BRUNO "Effondrer."

TEACHER Vous avez identifié les bons mots. Est-ce que quelqu'un sait ce que signifie "la rareté"? Sur une échelle de 1 à 5, dans quelle mesure êtes-vous d'accord avec l'affirmation suivante: Je sais ce que "la rareté" signifie…(attend les réponses des étudiants) Alors, Léo, tu as répondu 5. Peux-tu me donner la signification de "la rareté"?

LEO La rareté signifie "scarcity" en anglais.

TEACHER Très bien! Quelqu'un sait-il ce que signifie "la moyenne"? Sur une échelle de 1 à 5, dans quelle mesure êtes-vous d'accord avec l'affirmation suivante: Je sais ce que "la moyenne" signifie…*(attend les réponses des étudiants)* Oui, Ted?

TED Le mot la moyenne ne signifie-t-il pas "average" en anglais?

TEACHER Oui Ted, la moyenne est "average" en anglais.

TEACHER *(provides students with a piece of text about the humanitarian crisis in Venezuela)* Muy bien, observen el texto y echen un vistazo rápido para descubrir las palabras que no son familiares. Comiencen por la parte de abajo, lean hacia arriba y encierren con un círculo dos o más términos que no puedan definir.

(Students begin circling words on their handouts.)

TEACHER Bien, puedo ver que la mayoría de ustedes encontraron algunas palabras. Alessandra, dime una de las palabras que elegiste.

ALESSANDRA "La escasez."

TEACHER *(pauses and glances at poster)* Expresa tus pensamientos en oraciones completas.

ALESSANDRA Elegí la palabra "la escasez."

TEACHER *(writes down "la escasez" on dry erase board)* Gracias. Julia, ¿cuál fue una de las palabras que elegiste?

JULIA Elegí la palabra "el promedio."

TEACHER *(writes down the word "el promedio" on dry erase boa*rd) Bien, ¿alguien tiene alguna palabra que deberíamos incluir? ¿Leo?

LEO No estoy seguro de lo que es "deteriorar," pero sé que hablamos sobre eso.

TEACHER *(writes "deteriorar" on the board)* Escribamos eso también. ¿Alguna otra palabra?

BRUNO "Derrumbarse."

TEACHER Bien, estas son palabras excelentes. ¿Alguien sabe qué significa "la escasez"? Muéstrenme en una escala del 1 al 5 el grado en el cual estén de acuerdo con esta afirmación: Sé lo que significa "la escasez". ….*(espera a que los estudiantes respondan)* Bien, Leo, mostraste un 5. ¿Puedes decirme qué significa la escasez?

LEO La escasez significa "scarcity" en inglés.

TEACHER ¡Muy bien! ¿Alguien sabe qué significa "el promedio"? Muéstrenme en una escala del 1 al 5 el grado en el cual estén de acuerdo con esta afirmación: Sé lo que significa "el promedio"… *(espera a que los estudiantes respondan)* Sí, ¿Ted?

TED El promedio, ¿no significa "average" en inglés?

TEACHER Sí Ted, el promedio es "average" en inglés.

TEACHER *(provides students with a piece of text about the humanitarian crisis in Venezuela)* Okay, alle zusammen, lasst uns den Text betrachten und schnell nach unbekannten Begriffen suchen. Fangt an von unten nach oben zu suchen und kreist zwei oder mehr Begriffe ein, die ihr nicht erklären könnt.

(Students begin circling words on their handouts.)

TEACHER Okay, ich sehe die Meisten haben ein paar Begriffe gefunden. Alessandra, nenne mir einen der Begriffe, die du gefunden hast.

ALESSANDRA "Die Knappheit."

TEACHER *(pauses and glances at poster)* Bitte drücke deine Gedanken in einem vollständigen Satz aus.

ALESSANDRA Ich habe den Begriff "die Knappheit" gefunden.

TEACHER (writes down "die Knappheit" on dry erase board): Danke. Julia, welchen Begriff hast du gefunden?

JULIA Ich habe den Begriff "mittelmäßig" gefunden.

TEACHER *(writes down the word "mittelmäßig" on dry erase board)* Okay, hat sonst jemand einen Begriff, den wir aufführen sollten? Leo?

LEO Ich bin nicht sicher, was "verfallen" bedeutet, aber ich weiß, dass wir darüber gesprochen haben.

TEACHER *(writes 'verfallen' on the board)* Lasst uns das auch aufschreiben. Sonstige Begriffe?

BRUNO "Zusammenbruch."

TEACHER Okay, das sind großartige Begriffe. Weiß jemand, was "die Knappheit" bedeutet? Zeig mir auf einer Skala von 1-5 wie stark du dieser Aussage zustimmst: Ich weiß was "die Knappheit" bedeutet… *(wartet auf Antwort des Schülers)* Okay, Leo, du hast auf eine 5 gezeigt. Kannst du mir sagen, was "die Knappheit" bedeutet?

LEO Die Knappheit bedeutet "scarcity" auf Englisch.

TEACHER Sehr gut! Weiß jemand, was "mittelmäßig" bedeutet? Zeig mir auf einer Skala von 1-5 wie stark du dieser Aussage zustimmst: Ich weiß, dass "mittelmäßig" bedeutet… *(wartet auf Antwort)* Ja, Ted?

TED Bedeutet mittelmäßig nicht "average" auf Englisch?

TEACHER Ja, Ted, mittelmäßig bedeutet "average" auf Englisch.

While "Point and Talk" and "Scanning" enable students to acquire vocabulary through context, we can also develop students' vocabulary through specific vocabulary activities that help build comprehension. For example, in addition to the stem wall mentioned in Step 2. (see pgs. 66-67), many teachers of foreign languages find it helpful to regularly post vocabulary for students to use, called a "word wall." Whenever students write or talk, teachers refer to the word wall to facilitate student output using the new vocabulary. Word walls and word clouds can be made each time new vocabulary is introduced through authentic resources. These can be kept in student journals or written on large posters hung on the classroom walls. Graphic organizers are another tool that can be used to take in and process new vocabulary.

Making connections among multiple uses for the same vocabulary word is an important way to enhance input and a means of focusing on form. You can do this through a strategy called input flooding. Input flooding involves providing many examples of a certain vocabulary word or phrase along with visuals of each usage of the vocabulary word in different contexts that may change the meaning of the word or phrase. The teacher can guide the students through the examples or allow for quiet exploration of the vocabulary. Powerpoints, visual flip charts, sorting games, videos, and even a well-selected Google Image search are all effective tools for input flooding. Teachers who are engaged in technology-enhanced language learning might find that applications like Snapchat and Instagram provide an additional outlet for language exploration and input flooding. This technique works well with grammar, language function, culture, dialogue, and pronunciation in addition to vocabulary.

Activities that build vocabulary are important because they help students become more

comfortable using a broader range of words and structures as they learn to communicate about an increasing number of topics with fluidity. This increase in their ability to communicate boosts their confidence and understanding in the new language. The acquisition of vocabulary also helps students learn the functionality of language and recognize when words might change meaning depending on the content and context. Vocabulary activities that focus on having students comprehend and use new words in context help create a more interactive, language-rich classroom.

Remember our earlier discussion of language learning versus language acquisition (see pg. 24)? Language learning involves studying and memorizing the vocabulary and grammar of a target language. Students produce written and oral language and receive feedback from an instructor. Language acquisition involves receiving copious amounts of comprehensible input with low-stress opportunities for output in a target language. The only way for students to achieve high levels of fluency in a target language is by receiving sufficient amounts of oral and written input coupled with opportunities to express themselves in authentic contexts by speaking or writing. It is not possible to achieve proficiency by studying vocabulary and grammar alone.

For the AP® Foreign Language Course Instructor and the IB Diploma Programme Language Acquisition Instructor

Incorporating visuals and vocabulary strategies into your daily routine will allow you to provide comprehensible input and make access to language easier for your students. This is an extremely important aspect to introduce into your students' sphere of acquisition. As noted in the AP® course learning objectives for the interpretive mode of communication, students must be able to "synthesize information from a variety of authentic resources" (College Board, n.d., p. 16, 19). This is a test of their skills in the interpretive mode and how they are able to communicate to show comprehension of content and vocabulary as well as make connections or comparisons to certain text or audio/visual features and cultural aspects of the material (College Board, n.d., p. 17, 19-20). This includes students' ability to designate certain aspects of the content being studied as "practices, products, and perspectives," which is a requirement of the AP® course (College Board, n.d., p. 37). Students who score a 5 on the AP® exam and who will receive college credit for their AP® language course must proficiently use and respond with "culturally appropriate vocabulary and idiomatic expressions" (College Board, n.d., p. 13, 17, 20, 23, 27). One approach to this requirement is introducing visuals and vocabulary strategies that teach students how to integrate native speech into their everyday language.

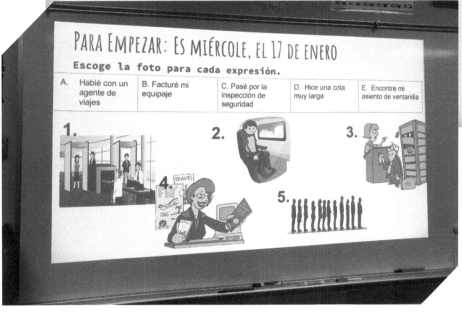

Photo courtesy of Frisco ISD

Motivation

☐ Giving students a point of reference: Students are more motivated when they are able to understand the language and topic. Visuals that are related to the language and topic will give students a point of reference to engage in the lesson and affirm their understanding of the content.

☐ Engaging students through use of gestures: The use of gestures and physical activity is motivating for students because it can get them out of their chairs and engaged with the content in a fun and relaxed way. This exercise can lower the affective filter and lead to higher engagement in and retention of language.

☐ Offering an opportunity for humor: Seeing the teacher acting in a silly manner lightens the atmosphere in the room, and students can be encouraged to join in on the fun and use gestures and movements to enliven their learning.

Access to Language

☐ Providing background knowledge and context to increase input: When students are provided with visuals and vocabulary strategies, they are receiving more sources of comprehensible input, which lead to greater understanding and comprehension in the target language.

☐ Increasing memory by using gestures: The research-based TPR approach (Asher, 1969) makes extensive use of gestures linking a demonstration of understanding to physical movement. When teachers link vocabulary words with gestures and physical movement, students are more likely to retain the vocabulary and access the learned words and phrases in the future.

☐ Creating expanded opportunities for output: When students are asked to repeat newly learned vocabulary, write a sentence using the new material, or read passages to scan for new words to later draw, discuss, or write about, they are engaged in practicing the four language domains (listening, speaking, reading, and writing). This enhances structured opportunities for both language input and production (output).

What additional research connects the use of targeted visuals and vocabulary instruction to increasing students' comprehension and language development?

The importance of providing comprehensible input through visuals and vocabulary instruction cannot be understated in a foreign language classroom. The success of instructional methods such as TPRS is credited to its reliance on the belief that all classes should be "comprehensible to all students" and also that these learners "must hear over and over the grammatical features and basic vocabulary that are essential for fluent expression of ideas" (Ray & Seely, 2015). TPRS is successful because the method focuses on comprehensible input. As Krashen states, "real language production happens only after the acquirer has built up competence via input" (1983, p. 298, as cited in Ray & Seely, 2015).

Visuals and vocabulary strategies also provide the learner with context for better comprehension. When students are reading in the target language, text can be made more comprehensible because of familiar words surrounding unknown words that help to create context. Studies have shown that higher-quality context surrounding new vocabulary words can increase meaning-making and understanding of new terms (Webb, 2008). When students lack context or have no idea what language is to come, their brains have to work extra hard to achieve comprehension. And even then, it may not be total comprehension.

Pre-teaching vocabulary enhances student reading comprehension. Stahl and Fairbanks (1986) demonstrate that student comprehension soars 33% when specific key terms are introduced prior to reading and learning (as cited in Marzano, Pickering, & Pollock, 2001).

Berlin, Germany

Photo courtesy of Anna Matis

FAQ

Photo courtesy of Anna Melis

Barcelona, Spain

SHOULD WE HAVE STUDENTS LOOK UP THE WORDS THAT HAVE BEEN SCANNED FROM A DICTIONARY AND HAVE THEM DEFINE THE WORDS ON THEIR OWN?

No. This will take too much time. Scanning is a quick process. Our goal is to give students the meaning of the scanned words within the context of what they are reading for that specific lesson or target language text. Having students look up isolated words in the dictionary does not meet this goal, because they will encounter multiple definitions riddled with more unfamiliar words.

WHY DOES THE SCAN PROCESS SEEM BACKWARD FOR MORE ADVANCED STUDENTS, GOING FROM THE END TO THE BEGINNING OF A PASSAGE?

Beginning the scan process from back to front helps advanced students focus on unfamiliar words and terms in the target language without reading the content. The unfamiliar words and terms will be more identifiable using the back-to-front process because it makes the scan procedure move along quickly.

THE VOCABULARY TECHNIQUES (LIKE SCANNING) ARE A NICE IDEA, BUT WILL THEY TAKE TOO MUCH TIME?

They do take time, but the time spent using these techniques is well worth the investment because student comprehension and understanding are increased. When students scan for unfamiliar words before reading a target language text, they will be more confident and successful during the reading task. When working with vocabulary in multiple ways, students gain a deeper understanding of the words, and they internalize the vocabulary's meaning.

SHOULDN'T WE DO SOMETHING MORE WITH VOCABULARY WORDS SO THAT STUDENTS WILL REALLY LEARN THEM?

Yes, we can put them on an interactive word wall posted in the classroom. A word wall is a place for word lists that change over time. On the word wall, we can list scan words from written material, key concepts, or words that might be helpful for students to use in writing or in conversation. Some of us put short definitions or translations next to the words, but others do not. The most important thing about word-wall words is to be sure that students have multiple opportunities to use the words when they write and speak in the target language.

1. Offer class and individual incentives for using the words and terms.

2. Require the use of specific words and terms in a warm-up writing assignment or in a reflective journal or exit ticket at the end of class.

3. Specify that a number of words and terms be used in written assignments during class for section reviews, written responses and short answers, or notes.

4. Encourage the use of specific words/terms in whole class or student-to-student conversation.

Step 5 ACTIVITIES

21. Point and Talk

DESCRIPTION

Point and Talk is a means of providing comprehensible input while explaining content and giving instructions to students in a foreign language class. This strategy involves teachers intentionally developing the habit of using gestures to reference posted language, visuals, and resources while giving directions to students and participating in whole class discussions.

DIRECTIONS

1. Preview a lesson and identify which directions you must give to students orally and what new vocabulary will be used.

2. Plan what objects you will refer to or hold to facilitate comprehensible input for the students while giving directions or using the new vocabulary.

3. When giving directions and/or using the new vocabulary, make sure to refer to the selected objects while making eye contact with students to gauge comprehension. If necessary, use response signals (for example, "Rate yourself on a scale of one to five showing how well you understand") to measure student understanding of the vocabulary and directions.

4. In addition, you can instruct students to utilize a series of signals to indicate when they need a slower pace, a resource such as a dictionary, or an opportunity to speak in English with a peer (e.g., forming a T with their hands to signal "time-out" or showing an outstretched palm when they need the teacher to slow down).

> Rate yourself on a scale of 1 to 5 showing how well you understand.

> Califícate en una escala del 1 al 5 para demostrar qué tanto entiendes.

> Évaluez votre niveau de compréhension sur une échelle de 1 à 5.

> Bewerte selbst auf einer Skala von 1 bis 5 wie gut dein Verständnis ist.

(Adapted from Seidlitz, Base, Lara, & Smith, 2016)

22. TPRS (Teaching Proficiency Through Reading and Storytelling)

DESCRIPTION

Using TPRS, teachers guide and facilitate the collaborative creation of a story with their students. Language teachers such as Blaine Ray and Ben Slavic developed this technique as a way of focusing on maximizing comprehensible input. Students learn new structures and vocabulary as the teacher embeds them into the story.

DIRECTIONS

1. The first step is to establish meaning. Select two to three new phrases that will compose the core of the story, and post these phrases/stems so they are clearly visible to the students. For example:

    ___ has/does not have _____.

    ___ wants/does not want ___.

    ___ goes to___.

    ___ a / n'a pas ____.

    ___ veut / ne veut pas ___.

    ___ va à ___.

    ___ tiene/no tiene _____.

    ___ quiere/no quiere _____.

    ___ va a___.

    _____hat/hat kein/e/en_____.

    ___ will/will nicht ___.

    ___ geht___.

2. Pronounce and clearly explain the meaning of the stems to the students. Then ask the students personal questions using the stems. For example, "Does Spencer have…?", "Does David want…?", "Does Tristan go…?"

3. The next step is to create a spoken class story in the target language. Do not so much tell the story as ask the students for the story. The stems will be repeated over and over as you ask the students about what happens to the character or characters next. Stems are often repeated between 50 and 100 times during this process. Students tend to remain engaged because of the humor and anticipation generated by deciding what happens next and contributing to the co-creation process from their own funds of knowledge and cultural framework.

TEACHER Greta does not have a dog. Greta does not have a cat. Greta does not have a horse. What does Greta have, Liesl?

LIESL Greta has a zebra.

TEACHER Greta has a zebra. Does Greta want a zebra? No Greta does not want a zebra. Greta wants… What does Greta want, Friedrich?

FRIEDRICH Greta wants a giraffe.

Step 5 ACTIVITIES

TEACHER Greta n'a pas de chien. Greta n'a pas de chat. Greta n'a pas de cheval. Liesl, quel animal Greta a-t-elle?

LIESL Greta a un zèbre.

TEACHER Greta a un zèbre. Greta veut-elle un zèbre? Non, Greta ne veut pas de zèbre. Greta veut…   Friedrich, que veut Greta?

FRIEDRICH Greta veut une girafe.

TEACHER Greta no tiene un perro. Greta no tiene un gato. Greta no tiene un caballo. ¿Qué es lo que tiene Greta, Liesl?

LIESL Greta tiene una cebra.

TEACHER Greta tiene una cebra. ¿Greta quiere una cebra? No, Greta no quiere una cebra. Greta quiere…   ¿Qué es lo que quiere Greta, Friedrich?

FRIEDRICH Greta quiere una jirafa.

TEACHER Greta hat keinen Hund. Greta hat keine Katze. Greta hat kein Pferd. Was hat Greta, Liesl?

LIESL Greta hat ein Zebra.

TEACHER Greta hat ein Zebra. Will Greta ein Zebra haben? Nein, Greta will kein Zebra haben. Greta will… Friedrich, was will Greta haben?

FRIEDRICH Greta will eine Giraffe.

4. The last step is for students to read a text containing the structures that they practiced. You may wish to read the story aloud and then have students work with a partner to translate the story or discuss its meaning in their native language. The goal is for students to have total comprehensibility of the passage.

(Adapted from Ray & Seely, 2015)

23. Scanning   *(Adapted from Seidlitz & Perryman, 2011)*

DESCRIPTION

Scanning is a strategy used to teach students essential words appearing in new content prior to reading. Students scan through a text backward in search of unfamiliar terms. The teacher provides an "in the moment" definition or explanation of the term that aids in comprehension.

DIRECTIONS

1. Have students survey a text looking for unfamiliar words. Beginners may start at the beginning of the document, trying to make sense of the text, noting words they simply can't make out. More advanced students can start at the bottom of a page and work up. Scanning the text backward helps advanced students quickly identify unfamiliar words without trying to read the material.

2. Ask students, as a class, to note the words they find. Then generate a list of three to ten unfamiliar terms from their lists. Students are able to discuss their predictions for what terms might mean before the teacher provides an explanation. This could sound like: "The term _____ is unfamiliar to me. I think it means…"

3. Students can write short, student-friendly definitions for the terms, making sure to give definitions that match the way the word is used in the context of the passage. **Note: The goal is to give students the information they need to understand the scan words they have listed. The goal is not for students to memorize or gain deep understanding of the words.

4. Practice pronouncing the terms with the students.

5. Ask students to read the passage.

6. Have students use the scan words to better understand classroom conversations and writing tasks related to the reading assignment.

Photo courtesy of Frisco ISD

Step 5 ACTIVITIES

24. Strategic TV

DESCRIPTION
Through guided discussion and demonstration, the teacher explains how students can use television and video to help them learn the target language more rapidly.

DIRECTIONS
1. Explain the concept of comprehensible input to your students, highlighting the fact that the more comprehensible input they receive in the target language, the faster they will develop proficiency in that language. Also explain the concept of compelling input, highlighting the fact that the more compelling people find the content, the more likely they are to watch it attentively.

2. Demonstrate to students how to watch TV and video strategically in order to increase comprehensible and compelling input, outlining the following key ideas:

   • Input will increase the more you understand the program you're watching.

   • Programs in which you have a high degree of interest are more likely to capture your attention and keep you watching for longer periods of time.

   • Watching recordings that you can pause and/or replay can increase comprehensible input. However, pausing too frequently can interrupt the flow necessary to receive large amounts of comprehensible input.

   • Utilizing closed captioning with the target language printed on the bottom of the screen can increase the amount of comprehensible input a viewer is receiving.

   • Some programs available online specialize in providing video-based comprehensible input for language learners (for example, YABLA, FluentU).

3. Provide a log for students to record the number of minutes watched and the programs viewed. You may wish to assign a particular genre of programming or a specific number of minutes for students to watch per day.

4. Provide opportunities in class for students to discuss the programs they are watching with one another, with the teacher, or with the entire class. Using sentence stems, students can speak or write about their experiences using Strategic TV.

(Adapted from Seidlitz, Base, Lara, & Smith, 2016)

25. Teach Cognates

DESCRIPTION

This activity helps students identify patterns of cognates from the target language to English by showing them examples. Cognates (and false cognates) exist in most foreign languages that our students are learning. Identifying cognates helps students identify similarities and differences between words in the target language and English and thus helps them reflect on what they know about language.

DIRECTIONS

1. Provide students with examples, and explain how cognates may be similar in the target language and English.

2. Put students in groups of four or five, and provide them with chart paper.

3. Have each group select one or two examples in the target language and English, and ask them to write their selection as a heading on their chart paper.

atractivo/iva	**attractive**
montañoso	**mountainous**
recientemente	**recently**
color	**color**
ansiedad	**anxiety**

4. Have students brainstorm a list, and ask them to color code the word endings to note differences as shown in the example below. Allow them to use books from the classroom library to locate more cognates.

5. Have students display their charts and add to them as more cognates are encountered in future lessons.

Example:

ivo/ive	oso/ous
atractivo – attractive	glorioso – glorious
intuitivo – intuitive	fabuloso – fabulous
creativo – creative	laborioso – laborious
activo – active	nervioso – nervous
decorativo – decorative	riguroso – rigorous
imaginativo – imaginative	nebuloso – nebulous

(Adapted from Seidlitz, Base, Lara, & Smith, 2016)

Step 5 ACTIVIES

26. Say It Another Way *(Adapted from Seidlitz & Kenfield, 2011)*

DESCRIPTION

This strategy for more advanced students enriches student vocabulary and increases the ability to use more varied and formal language (especially in writing). For this activity, teachers provide alternatives for a variety of words and phrases and then give students multiple opportunities to use those alternatives in writing and conversation. Using the "Say it Another Way Chart" helps students apply language they may not typically use.

DIRECTIONS

1. Create a chart with several columns.

   a. In the first column, list commonly found words or phrases that would be found in a writing example of the target language (examples from AP tests are particularly helpful).

   b. In the second, third, and fourth columns, list synonyms for each word or phrase in the first column. (See the samples below; one is an example in English, the other is a variation on the chart from a Spanish classroom in Frisco ISD). Be sure to make the chart large enough so that all students can see it clearly.

2. Have students write and converse using the more advanced vocabulary from the posted chart(s).

SAY IT ANOTHER WAY...

angry	irritated	livid	irate	fuming	furious	heated
happy	elated	contented	ecstatic	joyous	pleased	delighted
big	gigantic	massive	huge	enormous	colossal	gargantuan
small	minute	petite	undersized	diminutive	infinitesimal	miniature
easy	effortless	basic	simple	trouble-free	painless	straight-forward
difficult	challenging	intricate	obscure	complex	taxing	demanding
strange	outlandish	odd	atypical	unusual	bizarre	eccentric

Photo courtesy of Frisco ISD

27. Personal Dictionary (Quiz)

DESCRIPTION

A Personal Dictionary is a set of target language words written on index cards that students select for themselves and add to over time. Teachers often have students keep these Personal Dictionaries in index card boxes or ziplock bags. The Personal Dictionary Quiz provides teachers an opportunity for students to self-assess on the words they have selected.

DIRECTIONS

Set-up: Explain to students that after scanning a text (see pg. 113) for unknown words, they need to select at least two words to add to their personal dictionaries. Students will continue to add to this dictionary throughout a semester or school year. Once students have at least 20 cards in their dictionaries, tell the students they will be having a quiz on their personal dictionaries (pop-quiz or scheduled quiz).

1. Have students number a piece of paper one through ten.

2. Randomly partner students, and have them each select ten words out of their partner's box. Cards may be placed with either the English-word side or the target-language word side facing up.

3. Have students return to the ten words their partner selected.

4. Students will then write all ten words down, in both languages, without looking at the underside of the card.

5. Have students grade their own quizzes, and have them highlight on their papers any words they got incorrect.

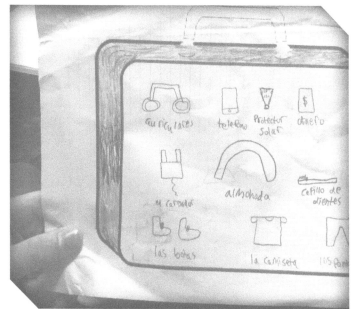

Photo courtesy of Frisco ISD

Lake Atitlán, Guatemala

STEP ⑥ *Have Students Participate in Structured Conversations*

What is Step 6?

Asking students to talk with each other using specific target language structures, phrases, and/or vocabulary about a clearly defined topic is called a structured conversation. Structured conversations allow students a chance to share ideas and points of view with each other. Not only are students participating in the interpersonal mode, but they are working through the ACTFL goal area of Communication to access the goal areas of Cultures, Comparisons, Connections, and Communities. When we are explicit about how students engage in discussion, it reduces a lot of the problems that arise when we ask students to work together in groups. During structured conversations, we see less off-task behavior, enhanced understanding of topics, and fewer classroom management problems.

Structured conversations can become a regular part of classroom instruction. Before setting up the structured conversation, it is important to make sure that students have enough background information and an adequate grasp of the content that will be discussed. We also want to be sure to model the process the first few times and ensure that students know which forms and structures in the target language they will be expected to use in the exercise.

Sometimes, we avoid using the strategy of structured conversation because we think it will take away valuable instructional time. However, structured conversations can be short — as little as 35 seconds or as long as five minutes if a topic really engages the students.

For example:

CHRIS I would like to visit Stockholm.

LAUREN But why? The weather is so cold there!

CHRIS Because I prefer cold weather. I love the snow! And you?

LAUREN I would like to visit Paris.

CHRIS Why do you want to visit Paris?

LAUREN Because I prefer walking in cities, seeing museums, and shopping. Oh, and eating the food!

CHRIS J'aimerais visiter Stockholm.

LAUREN Mais pourquoi? Il fait si froid là-bas!

CHRIS Parce que je préfère le froid. J'adore la neige! Et toi?

LAUREN J'aimerais visiter Paris.

CHRIS Pourquoi aimerais-tu visiter Paris?

LAUREN Parce que je préfère me promener en ville, voir des musées et faire du shopping. Ah oui, et goûter la nourriture locale!

CHRIS Me gustaría visitar Estocolmo.

LAUREN ¿Pero por qué? ¡El clima es tan frío allí!

CHRIS Porque prefiero el clima frío. ¡Me encanta la nieve! ¿Y a ti?

LAUREN Me gustaría visitar París.

CHRIS ¿Por qué te gusta visitar París?

LAUREN Porque prefiero caminar por las ciudades, visitar museos e ir de compras. Ah, ¡y comer las comidas!

CHRIS Ich würde gern Stockholm besuchen.

LAUREN Aber warum? Das Wetter ist so kalt dort!

CHRIS Weil ich kaltes Wetter bevorzuge. Ich liebe Schnee! Und du?

LAUREN Ich würde gern Paris besuchen.

CHRIS Warum würdest du gern Paris besuchen?

LAUREN Weil ich es vorziehe in der Stadt spazieren zu gehen, Museen zu sehen und einzukaufen. Oh, und das Essen zu essen!

Photo courtesy of Lamar CISD

Students have multiple opportunities to engage in structured conversations on a daily basis. This is especially true if students receive high-quality comprehensible input. Easy-to-implement examples include speaking with sentence frames, responding to text with a partner, and describing images with newly acquired vocabulary.

Teachers must facilitate these structured opportunities to allow students to practice. The teacher carrying the primary load of producing language output (i.e., talking, lecturing, and asking questions) "actually deprives learners of just those interactional features and conditions that research suggests are enabling factors in second language learning" (Gibbons, 2015, p. 32). On the other hand, when the teacher has effectively prepared the students to partake in structured conversations, research has suggested such student-to-student practice as being advantageous to whole group instruction. McGroarty's research (1993, as cited in

Gibbons, 2002, p. 17) offers the following three benefits:

1. Learners hear more language and a greater variety of language and have more language directed toward them; group-work situations increase the input to the learner.

2. Learners interact more with other speakers, and therefore their output is also increased. They tend to take more turns, and in the absence of the teacher, have more responsibility for clarifying their own meanings. In other words, it is the learners themselves who are doing the language learning work.

3. What learners hear and what they learn is contextualized: language is heard and used in an appropriate context and used meaningfully for a particular purpose.

This strategy will help you to reduce teacher talk time. An interactive, communicative classroom has much less teacher talk time than student talk time. Additionally, this takes some of the pressure off of teachers to produce the 90% target language usage in the foreign language classroom that is **recommended**

by ACTFL. *(https://www.actfl.org/news/position-statements/use-the-target-language-the-classroom)*

A simple strategy that weaves structured conversation into instruction is QSSSA (Question, Signal, Stem, Share, Assess).

What is QSSSA (Q, Triple S, A)?

This activity gets students using all four language domains of listening, speaking, reading, and writing in a fun and interactive manner. QSSSA is beneficial for language learners because it occurs in a low-stress environment where students have the wait time to negotiate meaning and practice responses with a partner before sharing orally with the class. Students are guided in their structured conversations by sentence stems and precise, easy-to-follow directions from the teacher.

In this strategy, the teacher asks a question, and the students give a response signal when they are ready to answer. Using a sentence stem, students are asked to share their responses with one or more peers. Lastly, the teacher assesses the quality of the discussion by selecting a few students to share their answers with the whole class. Students can also share by writing and then reading their responses. It is important for the teacher to use the randomize and rotate strategy to choose conversation partners so that students do not always have conversations with the same person or group of people next to them.

Q, Triple S, A

Question: Ask a question in the target language

Signal: Provide a way to indicate readiness

Stem: Provide a sentence starter for answering the question

Share: Give students an opportunity to share their responses with other students in pairs, triads, or groups

Assess: Randomly select students to respond, or ask everyone to write their responses

WHAT DOES EACH STEP OF QSSSA LOOK LIKE?

This structure begins with the teacher asking a question. The teacher can ask one question or a short series of questions for the students to respond to. When they have a response ready, students are then asked to provide a total response signal to indicate to the teacher and the class that they are ready to move on. This could be a hand in the air, pencil on paper, standing up, etc.

The teacher then provides a sentence stem for the students to use with a partner for sharing responses. The stem could be as simple as "I agree/disagree because_____."

The activity ends with the teacher assessing the students by randomly calling on a few to respond or rotating around to each group and asking for a response. QSSSA can also be a great way to help students practice the target language before writing.

See the chart on the next page for an example of the different variations of QSSSA in different language classes with varied response signals, sentence stems, and methods of formative assessment.

	QUESTION	SIGNAL	STEM	SHARE	ASSESS
English	What are you going to do in the summer?	Raise your hand when you can complete this sentence →	In the summer, I'm going to…	Share in groups of three	Randomly call on students who have June birthdays
Spanish	¿Qué vas a hacer en el verano?	Place your hand on your chin when you can complete this sentence → (Pon tu mano en la barbilla cuando puede completar esta oración)	Este verano voy a..	Numbered Heads Together	Randomly select groups and numbers to respond using index cards
German	Was werden Sie im Sommer tun?	Stand up when you can complete this sentence → (Steh auf, wenn du diesen Satz vervollständigen kannst)	Im Sommer…	Share in groups of two	Have students write their responses in journals
French	Qu'est-ce que vous allez faire en été?	Put your pen down when you can complete this sentence → (Posez votre stylo quand vous pouvez compléter cette phrase)	Je vais…cet été.	Share answers with several partners using appointment clocks	Chose student to randomly select from the stack of index cards with student names

Here's how a typical structured conversation might sound in the foreign language classroom:

TEACHER Which country has the largest French-speaking population outside of France? Please raise your hand when you can finish this sentence: The country with the largest French-speaking population outside of France is… *(Students all raise their hands)* Turn to the person next to you and say your complete sentence. If you agree with your partner, say: "I agree because…" If you disagree, say: "I disagree because…" Now turn to each other, and begin sharing. *(Students begin discussing)*

TEACHER Okay, which country has the largest French-speaking population outside of France? I'm going to draw a name….*(Teacher randomly selects a name from the stack of index cards)*... Steve?

STEVE The country with the largest French-speaking population outside of France is Canada.

TEACHER Thank you, Steve.

TEACHER Quel pays a la plus grande population francophone en dehors de la France? Levez la main si vous pouvez compléter cette phrase: Le pays ayant la plus grande population francophone en dehors de la France est...*(Students all raise their hands)* Tournez-vous vers votre voisin et prononcez la phrase complète. Si vous êtes d'accord avec lui, dites: "Je suis d'accord parce que…" Si vous n'êtes pas d'accord, dites: "Je ne suis pas d'accord parce que…" Maintenant, chacun se tourne vers son voisin pour lui donner sa réponse. *(Students begin discussing)*

TEACHER Alors, quel pays a la plus grande population francophone en dehors de la France? *(Teacher randomly selects a name from the stack of index cards)*... Steve?

STEVE Le pays ayant la plus grande population francophone en dehors de la France est le Canada.

TEACHER Merci, Steve.

TEACHER ¿Qué país tiene la población de habla hispana más grande fuera de México? Levanten la mano cuando puedan terminar esta oración: El país que tiene la población de habla hispana más grande fuera de México es. . . *(Students all raise their hands)* Diríjanse a la persona al lado suyo y digan su oración completa. Si estás de acuerdo con tu compañero, di: "Estoy de acuerdo porque…" Si no estás de acuerdo, di: "No estoy de acuerdo porque…"Ahora diríjanse entre sí y comiencen a compartir. *(Students begin discussing)*

TEACHER Bien, ¿qué país tiene la población de habla hispana más grande fuera de México? *(Teacher randomly selects a name from the stack of index cards.)*... Steve?

STEVE El país que tiene la población de habla hispana más grande fuera de México es Estados Unidos. "

TEACHER Gracias, Steve.

TEACHER Welches Land hat die größte Deutsch sprechende Bevölkerung außerhalb Deutschlands? Wenn du diesen Satz beenden kannst, melde dich bitte: Das Land mit der größten Deutsch sprechenden Bevölkerung außerhalb Deutschlands ist… *(Students all raise their hands)* Drehe dich zu deinem Nachbarn um und bilde einen vollständigen Satz. Wenn du deinem Partner zustimmst, sag: "Ich stimme zu, weil…" Wenn du nicht zustimmst, sag: "Ich stimme nicht zu, weil…" Dreht euch wieder einander zu und redet miteinander. *(Students begin discussing)*

TEACHER Okay, welches Land hat die größte Deutsch sprechende Bevölkerung außerhalb Deutschlands? *(Teacher randomly selects a name from the stack of index cards)…* Steve?

STEVE Das Land mit der größten deutsch sprechenden Bevölkerung außerhalb Deutschlands ist Österreich.

TEACHER Danke, Steve.

Here are examples of how content-area classrooms have successfully utilized QSSSA to facilitate structured conversations:

	QUESTION	SIGNAL	STEM	SHARE	ASSESS
Math	What are some important things to remember when factoring equations?	Raise your hand *when you can complete this sentence*	The most important thing to remember when factoring equations is… because…	Turn to your partner	Randomize when calling on students
Social Studies	Do you support Sam Houston's position on secession?	Place your hand on your chin *when you can complete this sentence*	I support/ oppose Sam Houston's position because…	Share with the group	Numbered Heads Together
Science	What are some unusual characteristics of annelids?	Stand up *when you can complete this sentence*	The most unusual characteristic of annelids is… because…	Turn to your partner	Randomize when calling on students
Language Arts	Is Stanley a hero?	Put your pen down *when you can complete this sentence*	Evidence that shows Stanley is/is not a hero includes …	Inside Outside Circle	Journal Reflection

For the AP® Foreign Language Course Instructor and the IB Diploma Programme Language Acquisition Instructor

Structured conversations as well as the reading and writing activities that you will read about in Step 7 are essential parts of your teaching toolkit. Heavy incorporation of these strategies is primary to achievement in upper levels of language acquisition. However, without practicing structured conversations (Step 6) and reading and writing activities (Step 7) as novice to intermediate language acquirers, your students will not arrive at the internal competence in the target language that they need to succeed on tests such as the IB or AP® exams. Structured conversations and reading and writing activities can easily be incorporated into the IB or AP® curriculum in order to access the themes, content, culture, and essential questions in each unit.

As noted in the AP® Curriculum Framework, "The Interpersonal Mode is characterized by active negotiation of meaning among individuals. Participants observe and monitor one another to see how their meanings and intentions are being communicated. Adjustments and clarifications can be made accordingly" (College Board, n.d., p. 7). This is exactly what your students will be doing in structured conversations. They will practice communication strategies such as "circumlocution, paraphrasing, restatement, and asking for clarification or information." They will be able to "recognize errors and self-correct" (College Board, n.d., p. 8-9, 13). They will be noticing language use and misuse as they practice recasting. They will "clarify and elaborate on content," and use a variety of "cohesive devices to report, explain, and narrate"(College Board, n.d., p. 22, 26). These are all parts of the AP® achievement level descriptions for level 4 & 5 in interpersonal and presentational communication. Students scoring a 4 are well qualified, and students scoring a 5 are extremely well qualified to receive college credit with the AP® exam.

Structured conversations provide the opportunity to communicate in the interpersonal mode and develop these competences, as well as provide strategies and awareness for successful presentational communication. Conversational competences also carry over to written competences, which are also practiced with Step 7.

When learners hear large amounts of comprehensible input and they are engaged in meaning-making, they understand and retain what they hear, and they use it to form their own messages (Long, 1981; Swain, 1995, as cited on ACTFL website).

HOW DOES STEP 6 PROVIDE STUDENTS WITH MOTIVATION AND ACCESS TO LANGUAGE?

Motivation

☐ Creating an interactive environment for learners: Students value environments where they get to interact with their peers. Incorporating structured conversations into each class period gives students the chance to interact with other students on a daily basis.

☐ Lowering the affective filter: Having students speak with their peers can mitigate a potential stressful opportunity if students are anxious about responding out loud in front of the whole class in those instances when they are nervous or unsure of the answer. The affective filter is lowered if they can first practice comfortably with a partner or group of students, and this practice is a motivator for students because they get to engage in learning and practice together.

☐ Increasing student proficiency in speaking: In order to be successful at anything in life, we have to devote time and willingness to practice. The more opportunities students have to practice speaking, the more they can increase their speaking proficiency. When students realize their proficiency is building, they can get a boost of confidence and motivation to go further.

Access to Language

☐ Providing an opportunity to receive input from other students: The interactive nature of structured conversations affords students the opportunity to hear various forms of input from their peers. Structured conversations are great for allowing students to talk in the target language about their personal preferences in things such as food, travel, or sports activities. Frequent use of structured conversations allows new and different vocabulary terms and phrases to circulate constantly. Students negotiate meaning by "turn-taking" and interacting with peers to make sense of the input (Hall, 2010).

☐ Noticing gaps beyond what they're currently able to express: When students speak with their peers, it is inevitable that speaking partners will have varying levels of abilities and recall of recently learned vocabulary, phrases, and structures. When students receive what Krashen (1982) calls a "more sophisticated" form of input (or i+1) from a speaking peer, students notice the gap between their perceived language level to that of their partner, and this can result in the production of more refined output in the target language (Swain, 1995).

☐ Offering students the chance to receive feedback from peers when other students recast: When the request to clarify output happens in the target language, students sometimes recast (see pg. 28) other students' responses. Students may sometimes do this automatically, but teachers can also explain recasting so that students can improve their structured conversations. Thus, structured conversation becomes an opportunity for students to receive clarification in the target language, which aids in comprehension and language production.

☐ Allowing students the opportunity to notice incorrect usage of language: Part of the awareness of correct language usage is being able to tell when someone else uses the language incorrectly. Thus, allowing the students to interact with each other and make mistakes not only allows the speaker the opportunity to notice their mistakes and self-correct, but it also allows the listener to notice incorrect language usage. This will solidify the correct language for the receivers and help them to not make the same mistakes.

What additional research shows the effect of structured conversations on students' comprehension and language development?

In previous sections, we have covered much of the research about the benefits of students producing output in the target language. Having students speak in a structured manner enables them to notice gaps in their abilities to produce certain sentences, phrases, and structure, that they wouldn't notice if they weren't practicing the speaking. This kind of interaction also gives students the practice of negotiation of meaning (Long, 1996). Until our students are in the midst of forming language in a conversation in the target language, they don't realize what they don't know!

Student-to-student interaction focused on lesson concepts has been shown to have a significant effect on student achievement (Marzano, Pickering, & Pollock, 2001). In several studies, students who participated in discussions with other students about a topic showed a percentile gain of 19 points over students who did not participate in discussions (Guzetti et al., 1993 as cited in Marzano et al., 2001). The use of sentence stems in structured conversations provides an opportunity to increase exposure to new vocabulary in the target language. Jenkins, Stein, and Wysocki

(1984) found that students need to be exposed to a word at least six times before they can remember its meaning. Structured conversations ensure that students get multiple exposures to target-language vocabulary and a chance to use new terms in an authentic context.

Vivian Cook (2008) encourages teachers to be mindful of their overuse of teacher talk, as this could undermine a communicative classroom by diminishing the back-and-forth structure that is used in the real world of communication. He describes the order that students are generally exposed to language as coming first from the teacher, second from the textbook or teaching materials, and third from other students in addition to sources outside the classroom. These all provide different types of language: the "genuine language of the classroom" from the teacher, the textbooks' purpose-designed inauthentic language (or authentic language taken out of its usual context), and the other students' interlanguage full of non-native-like forms, yet signifying genuine communication/interaction.

FAQ
FREQUENTLY ASKED QUESTIONS

Montreal, Canada

WHY SHOULD I USE STRUCTURED CONVERSATIONS LIKE QSSSA INSTEAD OF SIMPLY CALLING ON STUDENTS RANDOMLY IN THE CLASSROOM, ONE STUDENT AT A TIME?

First, structured conversations are much more engaging because the process includes 100% student participation. In single-student questioning, we select one student at a time to respond to a teacher's question while everyone else in the classroom remains passive. With structured conversations, every student must respond by completing the sentence stem given. QSSSA provides enough structure to get all students involved both physically and mentally. It maximizes "engagement" time in the classroom and minimizes single-student responses.

Introducing and training your students to use structured conversations such as QSSSA early in the school year or semester will get them accustomed to the process quickly.

WHAT HAPPENS IF STUDENTS WILL NOT PARTICIPATE IN THE STRUCTURED CONVERSATIONS?

Initially, there may be reluctance or hesitation by some students. Keep in mind that we are nudging our students from a very well-learned pattern of passivity into something that is much more engaging. Once students understand and have success with the process, they usually enjoy it and look forward to participating in it.

For students who need extra assistance, we simply provide a sentence in the target language to get them started. If need be, we give them an extra phrase to help them complete the given sentence stem. These additional sentence stems can be provided to students orally, in writing for the entire class to see, or on a notecard for their own personal use. Initially, we have to push and support the students as they become accustomed to structured conversations. With encouragement, support, and repetition, even our most reluctant students will soon feel comfortable and will join the process.

I DON'T UNDERSTAND THE "A" OF QSSSA.

The "A" of QSSSA stands for assess. The process is simple. After students have shared their completed sentence stems with a peer, the teacher can assess their responses by randomly calling on individual students. Students can share their sentence stems, or they can write about their learning experience during the structured conversation. This allows the teacher to assess responses and check student understanding. Teachers are not grading students; instead, they are using student responses to know whether to reteach or to move forward with the lesson. Other assessment methods include whole-class written responses or the Numbered Heads Together strategy with teams of students reporting their responses to the rest of the class.

DO WE HAVE THE TIME TO DO STRUCTURED CONVERSATIONS IN THE CLASSROOM?

First, let's stop and think about what we are currently doing with our students during the class period. Is it effective? What percentage of time are they actually speaking in the target language? What percentage of time during each class are our students engaged in learning? Are students in our classrooms actively involved, or are they sitting passively? How often do our students get the chance to verbalize and internalize the target language? What percentage of time are our students engaged in meaningful tasks using the target language?

Structured, accountable conversations take minimal preparation and are simple to implement. They enable us to engage students in learning in an active way while gaining practice in the target language.

I LIKE THE IDEA OF STRUCTURED CONVERSATIONS, BUT I'M NOT SURE MY STUDENTS WILL BE ABLE TO PARTICIPATE IN THEM.

Some students may initially resist participating in some of the conversation structures of an interactive classroom. In a foreign language classroom, we sometimes have to nudge them out of their passive "comfort zone" into a new "learning zone." If the conversations are properly implemented in a well-managed environment, students will be successful, and they will understand these conversations as a fun and effective way to learn a new language. On the first day of school, we should begin to nourish a climate of trust and expectation. When the process is introduced and carefully developed, students will become accustomed to the seven steps of an interactive, language-rich foreign language classroom.

Step 6 ACTIVITIES

28. QSSSA

DESCRIPTION

This strategy helps students use new target language structures and vocabulary during classroom conversations. The teacher asks the essential question that will be addressed in the conversation. Students give a signal when they are ready to respond and are given a sentence stem to use for their response. After sharing with a partner, students are chosen randomly to share with the whole group. In this activity, every student in the class participates using academic language, and it usually takes less than a minute to implement.

QUESTION: Ask the class a question.

SIGNAL: Ask students to give you a response signal when they are ready to answer the question.

STEM: Provide students with a sentence stem to use when answering a question.

SHARE: Give students an opportunity to share their responses with other students in pairs, triads, or groups.

ASSESS: Determine the quality of student discussions and the level of understanding by randomly selecting students to share out loud or by having all students write a response.

(Adapted from Seidlitz & Perryman, 2011)

	QUESTION	SIGNAL	STEM	SHARE	ASSESS
English	What are you going to do in the summer?	Raise your hand when you can complete this sentence →	In the summer, I'm going to…	Share in groups of three	Randomly call on students who have June birthdays
Spanish	¿Qué vas a hacer en el verano?	Place your hand on your chin when you can complete this sentence → *(Pon tu mano en la barbilla cuando puedas contestar esta oración.)*	Este verano voy a…	Numbered Heads Together	Numbered Heads Together
German	Was werden Sie im Sommer tun?	Stand up when you can complete this sentence → *(Steh auf, wenn du diesen Satz vervollständigen kannst.)*	Im Sommer…	Share in groups of two	Have students write their responses in journals
French	Qu'est-ce que tu vas faire l'été prochain?	Put your pen down when you can complete this sentence → *(Posez votre stylo quand vous pouvez compléter cette phrase.)*	Je vais…cet été.	Share answers with several partners using appointment clocks. Chose student to randomly select from the stack of index cards with student names	Chose student to randomly select from the stack of index cards with student names

Step 6 ACTIVITIES

29. Conversation Structures

DESCRIPTION

Classroom management can be tricky when you have 25 or more students working in groups. Sometimes it borders on chaotic, but with a little bit of planning, teachers can structure student interactions so they are controlled, productive, and fun. The ideas listed on this page give students multiple opportunities to discuss the academic concepts of each day's lesson in an organized way.

DIRECTIONS

Lines of Communication: Students form two lines facing one another. The students in each row share ideas, review concepts, or ask one another questions. After the first discussion, one row moves, and the other row remains stationary so that each student now has a new partner (Echevarria, Vogt, & Short, 2017).

Carousel: Questions are posted in various stations around the room. Students are assigned to groups, and each group is assigned to a station and given a specified time to answer the questions at the station. Groups rotate around the room until everyone has answered all questions (Santa, Havens, & Valdes, 2004).

Fold the Line: Students line up chronologically based on a predetermined characteristic such as height, age, number of pets, etc. The line then folds in half upon itself, providing each student with a partner. Partners are then asked to formulate a response to a given task or question (Kagan & Kagan, 2009).

Think, Pair, Share: The teacher asks a question and then provides wait time. The students formulate answers and then share the answers with their partners. Afterward, selected students share their thoughts with the whole class (Lyman, 1981).

Inside/Outside Circle: Students form two concentric circles facing one another — an inside circle and an outside circle. Students then participate in a short, guided discussion or review with their partner. After the discussion, the outside circle rotates to the right while the inside circle remains still. Each student now has a new partner for discussion (Kagan & Kagan, 2009).

Gallery Walk: Questions, prompts, or tasks to be completed are posted in various stations around the room. Students are assigned to a group, and each group is assigned to a station and given a specified time to answer the question or complete the task at the station. Groups rotate around the room until each group has visited every station.

30. Talk Show

DESCRIPTION
Students participate in a talk show where they represent the views of various characters from a vocabulary or literary unit.

DIRECTIONS

1. Choose a topic for a series of talk shows that students can perform in groups. For example, if studying Christmas traditions in a German class, students can choose from: "Christkind und Weihnachtsmann? Oder Krampus und Schwarzer Peter?", "Weihnachtslieder", "Stollen oder Lebkuchen?", and "Der Tannenbaum."

2. In small groups, students can prepare an improvised talk show about their topic. They must choose a host, identify characters, prepare questions to ask, and write possible responses. The group can choose to allow audience questions if they wish. Students are encouraged to use humor and surprise but to avoid anachronisms.

Ladies and Gentlemen, welcome to...

- **Our topic today is...**
- **We have _____ with us...**
- **Now, for our first question...**
- **The last question for our guests is...**

Mesdames et messieurs, bienvenue à...

- Le thème du jour est...
- Nous avons _____ avec nous...
- Maintenant, pour notre première question...
- La dernière question à poser à nos invités est...

Damas y caballeros, bienvenidos a...

- Nuestro tema de hoy es...
- Tenemos a _____ con nosotros...
- Ahora, nuestra primera pregunta...
- La última pregunta para nuestros invitados es...

Meine Damen und Herren, willkommen...

- Unser Thema heute ist...
- Wir haben_____ mit uns...
- Nun zu unserer ersten Frage...
- Die letzte Frage an unsere Gäste lautet...

(Adapted from Seidlitz & Perryman, 2011)

Step 6 ACTIVITIES

31. Prop Box Improvisation

DESCRIPTION
Students use props to create a verbal and visual representation of text.

DIRECTIONS
After reading and studying a given topic/unit, students use a box of props to improvise and role-play assigned scenes related to the newly completed topic. For example, after reading and studying ordering and eating at a restaurant, organize students into four teams. Each team will be responsible for developing an improvisation of a dining experience. The challenge for each team is to use as many props as possible and to incorporate as many details and vocabulary words as they can in the improvisation/role-play.

A narrator can be chosen to narrate each presentation. Students must use at least one vocabulary word during the performance. After each presentation, debrief by asking the audience to note the content details and the effective use of props. Provide the sentence frames below for students to frame their responses.

Suggested props for Prop Box: feathers, binoculars, sunglasses, canteens, swords, scarves, artificial flowers, crosses, colored cloth fabric, markers, construction paper, bandanas, canes, crowns, jewelry, plastic food, table settings, and rope. (Note: swords, binoculars, crown, jewelry, etc. are all plastic and all toys.)

- They demonstrated _____ using...
- They showed _____ with...
- I think they were trying to show ___ using...
- They represented...

- Ils ont prouvé _____ à l'aide de...
- Ils ont montré _____ avec...
- Je pense qu'ils essayaient de montrer ___ à l'aide de...
- Ils ont décrit...

- Lo demostraron _____ utilizando...
- Lo mostraron _____ con...
- Creo que intentaban demostrar ___ utilizando...
- Representaron...

- Sie haben _____ gezeigt, durch Verwendung von...
- Sie haben _____ mit... gezeigt.
- Ich denke, sie wollten ___ durch Verwendung von... zeigen.
- Sie haben... dargestellt.

(Adapted from Seidlitz & Perryman, 2011)

32. Problem-Solution Teams

DESCRIPTION

In this activity students are provided an opportunity to become invested in the target language community by engaging with current events, discussing issues, and presenting possible solutions.

DIRECTIONS

1. Choose an article on a contemporary issue which the students could propose possible solutions for business leaders, political leaders, or members of the community.

2. Form students into small groups of three to five students.

3. Pass out the article to the students.

4. Explain to the students that they will have 20 minutes to prepare talking points in the target language on ways to address the issue discussed in the article. Students may use dictionaries or translation devices to help them understand the article and to prepare their talking points.

5. Tell the students that their presentations must meet the following criteria:

a. Each group member must share at least one complete sentence. Stems may include the following:

This article discussed...	L'article parlait de...
This is a problem because...	C'est un problème parce que...
Our group thinks we can address this problem by...	Notre groupe pense que nous pouvons résoudre ce problème en...
This would include.../This would involve...	Il faudrait notamment... / La solution implique de...

Este artículo hablaba sobre...	In diesem Artikel geht es um...
Esto resulta ser un problema porque...	Dieses ist ein Problem, da...
Nuestro grupo piensa que podemos abordar este problema al...	Unsere Gruppe denkt, dass wir dieses Problem durch... angehen können.
Esto incluiría.../Esto incluiría...	Dies würde .... beinhalten/ Dies würde.... involvieren.

b. Each group must prepare a poster listing their talking points. Poster may include drawings that represent their talking points.

Step 6 ACTIVITIES

6. Explain to groups that after each presentation, there will be an opportunity for question and answer. The teacher and fellow students may ask questions, including the meanings of words used during the presentation. Presenters need to be prepared to respond to questions and stems such as these:

I didn't understand...

What does the word ____ mean?

Why do you think...?

Is there another...?

Could you please tell me more about...?

Je n'ai pas compris.

Quelle est la signification du mot____?

Pourquoi pensez-vous....?

Il y a un/une autre...?

Pouvez-vous me donner plus d'information sur...?

No entendí...

¿Qué significa la palabra...?

¿Por qué piensas...?

¿Hay otro/otra...?

¿Me podrías decir más acerca de...?

Ich habe...nicht verstanden.

Was bedeutet das Wort...?

Warum denken Sie...?

Gibt es noch einen...?/Gibt es eine andere...?

Könnten Sie mir bitte mehr über ... erzählen?

7. After all groups have presented, have students write individual paragraphs describing a strategy for addressing the issue discussed in the article.

EXTENSION ⟶ *For advanced levels, make Step 4 a Timed Talk (see pg. 137).*

33. Timed Talk

DESCRIPTION

In this discussion strategy, students are given a set time during which they must use the target language to meet a group goal.

DIRECTIONS

1. Plan a cooperative task for students (three to five students per group), such as creating a poster, designing an ad, or writing talking points for a discussion.

2. Explain to the students that for 20 minutes they will only be allowed to use the target language (the teacher can vary time length based on class proficiency). Students may use dictionaries and translation devices for themselves, but they may not show each other their devices during the activity.

3. After completing the task, groups will present their finished product using the target language. All students in each group must speak at some point during the presentation.

Photo courtesy of Frisco ISD

(This extension activity, as well as "Problem-Solution Teams" on pg. 135 were inspired by Kimberly Church and her Spanish II students at Lebanon Trails HS, Frisco ISD)

Step 6 ACTIVITIES

34. T-Chart, Pair, Defend

DESCRIPTION

In this activity, the teacher has students participate in a conversation from two different points of view.

DIRECTIONS

1. Choose a vocabulary-rich text that will enable students to have a conversation from two different points of view.

2. Select a pair of characters related to the text who could have two different points of view.

3. Have students read and annotate the text.

4. Have students brainstorm possible attitudes and beliefs of the two selected characters from the text on a T-chart.

5. Have students form pairs and take turns role-playing the two characters in conversation. Characters could be travelers making a decision, weathermen debating a forecast, or characters from a novel or short story. The conversation always begins with a structured sentence frame like the following:

We should.../We shouldn't... It is.../It isn't... It is important.../It is not important...	Nous devrions... / Nous ne devrions pas... C'est... / Ce n'est pas... Il est important de... / Il n'est pas important de...
Deberíamos.../No deberíamos... Es.../No es... Es importante.../No es importante...	Wir sollten.../ Wir sollten nicht... Es ist.../Es ist nicht... Es ist wichtig/ Es ist nicht wichtig...

EXTENSION → *The teacher may select volunteers to perform their dialogues in front of the class and then follow with a class discussion.*

(Adapted from Seidlitz & Perryman, 2011)

35. Perspective Choice *(Adapted from Seidlitz & Perryman, 2011)*

DESCRIPTION

Students engage in dialogue from different perspectives as they take part in a group of six people who must make choices.

DIRECTIONS

1. After reading and discussing a topic, select a situation in which a group of six people must make a decision. Examples include a group of friends deciding what to do that night, a family picking recreational activities for their vacation, or a group of travelers trying to decide how to handle a missed connection.

2. As a class, use the sentence frames listed below to write six different sentences that represent different perspectives on the same event using the sentence stems listed below.

   For example:

"I think we should go to the movie theater because we've never seen this movie before."

"Perhaps we should to go to the mall because we will be able to visit some of the new stores and buy clothes."

"It would be a good idea to go swimming because it is a fun and healthy thing to do."

"We definitely shouldn't go biking, because it is about to rain."

"It's not wise to go to the club, because there are too many gangs on that street."

"I don't believe it's a good idea to go out at all, because we have too much school work to do for tomorrow."

"Je pense que nous devrions aller au cinéma parce que nous n'avons pas encore vu ce film."

"Peut-être que nous devrions aller au centre commercial pour découvrir les nouvelles boutiques et acheter des vêtements."

"Ce serait une bonne idée d'aller nager parce que c'est amusant et bon pour la santé."

"Nous ne devrions vraiment pas faire une promenade à vélo car il va pleuvoir."

"Ce n'est pas prudent d'aller à la boîte de nuit car il y a trop de voyous dans cette rue-là."

"Je ne crois pas que ce soit une bonne idée de sortir, parce que nous avons trop de devoirs pour demain."

"Creo que debemos ir al cine porque nunca vimos esta película."

"Quizás deberíamos ir al centro comercial porque podremos visitar algunas de las tiendas nuevas y comprar ropa."

"Sería una buena idea ir a nadar porque es divertido y muy saludable."

"Definitivamente no deberíamos ir a andar en bicicleta porque está por llover."

"No es aconsejable ir al club porque hay demasiadas pandillas en esa calle."

"No creo que sea una buena idear salir porque tenemos que hacer mucha tarea para la escuela para mañana."

"Ich denke wir sollten ins Kino gehen, weil wir diesen Film niemals zuvor gesehen haben."

"Vielleicht sollten wir ins Einkaufszentrum gehen, weil wir dort einige der neuen Läden besuchen und Kleidung kaufen können."

"Es wäre eine gute Idee schwimmen zu gehen, weil es Spaß macht und gesund ist."

"Wir sollten definitiv nicht Fahrradfahren, weil es gleich anfängt zu regnen."

"Es ist nicht klug in den Club zu gehen, weil auf der Straße zu viele Gangs sind."

"Ich glaube nicht, dass es eine gute Idee ist überhaupt auszugehen, weil wir zu viele Hausaufgaben für morgen aufhaben."

Step 6 ACTIVITIES

3. Number the perspectives one through six and have students form small groups of six, each student taking a different perspective.

4. Students begin by reading a sentence from the board and then improvising a conversation based on their impression of what the characters might say.

5. Students may repeat their conversations as a class. The class as a whole can then discuss what might be the best choice for the group.

- I think we should _____ because...
- Perhaps we should _____ because...
- It would be a good idea to...
- We definitely shouldn't _____ because...
- It's not wise to _____ because...
- I don't believe it is a good idea to _____ because...

- Creo que deberíamos _____ porque...
- Quizás deberíamos _____porque...
- Sería una buena idea...
- Definitivamente no deberíamos _____ porque...
- No es aconsejable _____ porque...
- No creo que sea una buena idea _____ porque...

- Je pense que nous devrions _____ parce que...
- Peut-être que nous devrions _____ parce que...
- Ce serait une bonne idée de...
- Nous ne devrions certainement pas _____ parce que...
- Ce n'est pas prudent de _____ parce que...
- Je ne crois pas que ce soit une bonne idée de _____ parce que...

- Ich denke wir sollten _____ weil...
- Vielleicht sollten wir _____, weil...
- Es wäre eine gute Idee zu...
- Wir sollten definitiv nicht_____, weil...
- Es ist nicht klug_____, weil...
- Ich glaube nicht, dass es eine gute Idee ist _____, weil...

STEP ⑦ Have Students Participate in Structured Reading and Writing Activities

Town of Chefchaouen, Morocco

What is Step 7?

When students can establish a literacy practice in the target language by reading and writing in class, they are well on their way to building a successful foundation for language development. Step 7 is about structuring these reading and writing activities so that students have extensive opportunities for practice while gaining a deeper understanding of vocabulary and language structures.

Structured Reading Activities

Language learners may acquire more high-level vocabulary and language structures when they read comprehensible texts than when they simply engage in conversations in the target language with their peers. This occurs because written language typically includes more low-frequency vocabulary and more complex language structures than we use in a social conversation. This is why we have students read both texts that we as teachers select and texts they select themselves.

TEACHER-SELECTED TEXT

Selecting Texts
There are a variety of places to find foreign language texts for students to read. The state-adopted or school/program-selected textbook can be a primary source of input. Additionally, sources of published literature (either selected by the teacher or required by the curriculum) such as poetry, short stories, and/or novels are common sources of input.

As students gain comprehension, an important source of input is authentic text in the target language, especially if it's procured from the country or countries where the target language is spoken. Authentic texts are any kind of written material produced with the native speaker as the intended audience. Examples of authentic texts could include newspapers, maps, restaurant menus, and TV show subtitles. These publications and examples have to be real — not produced for a foreign-language-learning or classroom audience. If the teacher modifies any of these examples in print, they are no longer "authentic" and should be classified as adapted text or teacher-produced input. As students gain more fluency, they become more successful comprehending unmodified, authentic text.

Authentic resources provide a limitless amount of interpretive listening and reading material for the foreign language classroom. With the help of a simple graphic organizer, students can access language at a level slightly above their own and acquire new language in chunks (more on graphic organizers on the next page). This allows teachers to use theoretical knowledge of second language acquisition and put it into practice with ease. However, to use authentic resources effectively in the LOTE classroom, the teacher must consider several aspects of each resource.

Who is the intended audience, and what is the purpose of the resource?

What characteristics of the resource are challenging?

How will I scaffold the resource to make it accessible to my students?

What strategies will my students use to access the information being presented?

What kind of graphic organizer can I employ to allow my students to interpret and interact with the authentic resource?

How will my students use learned language in a follow-up activity?

By planning lessons around these questions, we are able to move our students from ACTFL's interpretive mode to the interpersonal and presentational modes. It becomes easier for us to identify challenges students may face in an immersive use of genuine, unaltered resources. We can then prepare our students by helping them to identify their prior knowledge of a given topic.

It is unlikely that we will find the "perfect" authentic resource. But we can always be flexible, even when we can't find a resource that perfectly fits our students' current language proficiency level. The goal is to challenge our students by allowing them to work at a higher level than an adapted resource, like a textbook.

Processing Texts

All teacher-selected reading activities should be purpose-driven. In other words, we should be able to answer this question: Why am I having my students read this? Once the purpose for the reading activity is defined, we need to make a plan. Asking, "How will I make sure my students are ready to read this?" helps the planning process. We need to decide whether students are ready to read the text independently; if they are not, we need to put supports in place to ensure success. To prepare students to read independently, we can establish prior knowledge related to the reading assignment, scan the text for unfamiliar words (see pg. 100), or allow students to engage in a shared reading activity, such as partner-reading the text.

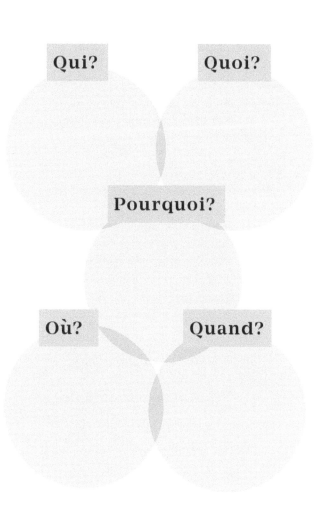

Another effective visual tool for processing text is the graphic organizer. By breaking the language into smaller chunks with simple tasks and graphic organizers, our students will learn and internalize vocabulary and language use through action rather than memorization. These activities help students learn by reinforcing strategies for accessing language. Follow-up activities allow students to use the language they learned individually during the activity.

To the right is an example of a graphic organizer designed by Elizabeth Johnson for a French class, which can easily be adapted for any target language:

SELF-SELECTED TEXTS

There is an incredible amount of power in letting language learners self-select their text for reading. One approach for encouraging this in the foreign language classroom is by adopting free voluntary reading as a norm and practice. Free Voluntary Reading (FVR) is a research-based approach to encourage students to independently read target-language texts. The approach involves teachers providing students with specific amounts of time to engage in reading texts that the students self-select. FVR programs have been demonstrated to be one of the most powerful ways to increase students' language development in the target language (Krashen, 2011).

This approach has been proven to get learners deeply engaged in the reading process and help them truly build a love of reading. This means students are excited not only about reading itself but also about what they are reading. As teachers, our goal is to provide students with choices of high-interest text that is engaging enough to "hook" our students but is at a reading level commensurate with the students' own reading abilities.

> The optimal experience of flow as a theory of motivation is one that has the power to promote reading as a regular and established practice for learners (Csíkszentmihályi, 2009).

For any self-selected reading approach like FVR to be successful, it must be structured such that teachers focus on helping students find books they want to read. It is also important to structure this time in ways that have been proven successful. For example, students are more likely to engage in reading when they know they will have a specific opportunity to speak with a peer or the teacher about what they are reading.

Here are some guidelines adapted from Bamford and Day (2004) for building an extensive reading program like FVR in the language classroom:

1. The reading material is easy and accessible. For students to be successful, the process of reading in the second language should not cause them to struggle. This may mean reducing the amount of new vocabulary in a piece of text so that students feel comfortable attaining meaning. Some publishers produce material that is designed for second language learners at low reading levels. Examples include: TPRS Publishers, BBC Mundo, Mary Glasgow Magazines, Newsela Español, etc.

2. Reading material can come in various forms and on a wide array of topics. Such variety ensures that students have ample texts to choose from that match their interest levels. Various texts can also serve different purposes, such as to entertain or even to expand learning on a cultural topic.

3. Learners choose what they want (and don't want) to read. This is the cornerstone of self-selection. Students remain engaged when they select text according to their own interests. Inherent for this step to work is the understanding that students can choose to stop reading a selection if they no longer deem it interesting.

4. Learners read as much as possible. This is where book length comes in to play, as beginner readers should start off with shorter length texts to ensure engagement and understanding.

5. Reading speed tends to be faster. Given that the text is self-selected, highly engaging, and easy for the student to understand, reading speed can increase as students gain fluency. Bamford and Day suggest offering texts in which students do not have to rely on dictionary use, as this can impede the flow of reading. Instead students are encouraged to guess or use context clues to deduce meaning.

6. The purpose of reading is usually related to pleasure, information, and general understanding. This is an interesting contrast to academic reading, for not only is self-selected text intended to be entertaining and possibly informative, but students need only understand the gist to move on.

7. Reading is individual and silent. For this to be effective, teachers need to set aside time during class for students to engage in reading. A suggested time is 20 minutes, although this may need to occur in gradual intervals as students build fluency. Additionally, self-selected reading is a wonderful supplement to homework.

8. Reading is its own reward. Extensive reading opportunities are generally not followed with comprehension questions, for as Bamford and Day put it, "a learner's own experience is the goal" (2004, p.3). Instead, follow-up activities can serve the purposes of finding out what students learned and their attitudes toward the reading — all with the general goal of encouraging rather than discouraging reading.

9. The teacher sets the purpose for reading. He or she does this by orienting and guiding the students and explaining why they are reading. Building on the above-mentioned guideline, teachers will want to follow up with the students to keep track of what and how much they read, as well their attitudes and reactions toward the reading.

10. The teacher must model reading. For this to be successful, the teacher must serve as a role model for the reading process, and students must see the teacher engaged in reading similar texts in the classroom setting. This practice offers students buy-in when the teacher recommends certain texts based on interest. Bamford and Day share that this process can lead the teacher and students in becoming an "informal reading community, experiencing together the value and pleasure to be found" in reading (2004, p. 3).

Structured Writing Activities

Two types of writing in the foreign language classroom are essential to creating a language-rich, interactive classroom: shared writing and independent writing. Shared writing occurs when students collaborate with one another and the teacher to create a text in the target language. Shared writing enables students to receive support from the teacher and their peers as they experiment with new vocabulary and language structures. Independent writing serves a different purpose. It provides students opportunities to grow in confidence and fluency in the target language. As students learn that they are capable of independently producing text, they become more willing to interact with their peers, both verbally and in writing. Below are samples of structures for shared writing and independent writing that can be frequently used in foreign language classrooms.

SHARED WRITING STRUCTURES

Independent Writing with Collaboration

For language learners, it is essential to practice speaking and writing in the target language, especially in an environment that lowers the affective filter (see pg. 26) and enhances the ability to produce low-stress output. Independent writing with collaboration is successful when teachers use various grouping structures and opportunities to engage in structured conversation as part of the writing experience. It can be as simple as having students think through what they want to write with a partner before creating their own text in the target language. Teachers can also use more complex structures that enable students to interact with a variety of peers before writing. For example, in Roving Paragraph Frames (see pg. 73) teachers have students engage in a series of conversations with a variety of partners as they independently create their own paragraphs.

Creating Text as a Class

Working together to create a text as a classroom community can provide opportunities for teachers to model correct target language usage and the thinking involved in writing in a target language. To create a text as a class, teachers can begin with a single sentence stem and take input from the students about how to complete it. Teachers can then prompt students to create new sentences and stems to expand on the initial sentence. It's important to keep having students participate in structured conversation and using randomizing strategies to keep them all engaged throughout these activities.

INDEPENDENT WRITING STRUCTURES

Scaffolded Paragraph Frames

Providing sentence stems and paragraph frames is key to scaffolding writing opportunities for all students learning a new language. Stems and frames not only support language structures but they can also help provide emergent writers with springboards for expressing their thoughts in complete sentences. Teachers can effectively use Jeff Zwiers' Academic Paragraph Frames as a model to create their own paragraph frames. He has several examples of academic paragraph frames on his website.

Jeff Zwiers – Academic Paragraph Frames

http://www.ouhsd.k12.ca.us/wp-content/uploads/docs/migrant_paragraph_frames.pdf

In more advanced classes, teachers can collaborate with students to create frames before students engage in writing. The following are examples of paragraph frames to use in the foreign language classroom:

1. Writing a complaint

I'm writing to let you know.....

This was a problem because...

I would like you to....

Example. I'm writing to let you know that the airline lost my luggage. This was a problem because I had an important business meeting in the morning. I would like you to address this situation.

Je vous écris pour vous informer que...

C'était un problème parce que...

Je voudrais que vous...

Example. Je vous écris pour vous informer que la compagnie aérienne a perdu ma valise. C'était un problème parce que j'avais une réunion d'affaires importante le matin. Je voudrais que vous régliez ce problème.

Estoy escribiendo para informarle ...

Esto resultó un problema porque...

Me gustaría que usted...

Example. Estoy escribiendo para informarle que la aerolínea perdió mi equipaje. Esto resultó un problema porque tenía una reunión importante de negocios por la mañana. Me gustaría que se encargue de esta situación.

Ich schreibe, um mitzuteilen, dass...

Dieses war ein Problem, da...

Ich würde gern...

Example: Ich schreibe, um mitzuteilen, dass die Fluggesellschaft mein Gepäck verloren hat. Dies war ein Problem, da ich am Morgen ein wichtiges Geschäftstreffen hatte. Ich würde diese Situation gern ansprechen.

2. Persuasion

We should….

The first reason we should…is

Another reason…

Finally we should…. because….

Example. We should visit Barcelona. The first reason we should visit Barcelona is to see the architecture. Another reason to visit Barcelona is for the spectacular art. Finally, we should visit Barcelona to try tapas and other local Spanish food.

Nous devrions…

La première raison pour laquelle nous devrions… est

Une autre raison…

Enfin, nous devrions… parce que…

Example. Nous devrions visiter Barcelone. La première raison pour laquelle nous devrions visiter Barcelone est d'admirer l'architecture. Une autre raison de visiter Barcelone est de découvrir l'Art nouveau. Enfin, il faut visiter Barcelone pour goûter les tapas et les autres plats régionaux d'Espagne.

Deberíamos...

El primer motivo por el que deberíamos... es

Otro motivo...

Por último, deberíamos... porque...

Example. Deberíamos visitar Barcelona. El primer motivo por el que deberíamos visitar Barcelona es para ver la arquitectura. Otro motivo para visitar Barcelona es por su arte espectacular. Por último, deberíamos visitar Barcelona para probar las tapas y otra comida local española.

Wir sollten...

Der erste Grund, warum wir... sollten ist...

Ein weiterer Grund...

Letztendlich sollten wir...weil...

Example: Wir sollten Barcelona besuchen. Der erste Grund, warum wir Barcelona besuchen sollten ist, um die Architektur zu sehen. Ein weiterer Grund Barcelona zu besuchen ist die spektakuläre Kunst. Letztendlich sollten wir Barcelona besuchen, um Tapas und das lokale spanische Essen zu probieren.

3. Description

.......is interesting because......

In addition....

For example....

Also....

Example. Tamales are interesting because they are a very popular food in Latin America. In addition, tamales are available in a variety of flavors. For example, in Mexico, they make tamales with corn husks, and in Central America they make them with banana leaves. Also, people fill tamales with various meats, fruits, spices, and cheeses.

... est intéressant parce que ...

En plus...

Par exemple...

Et aussi...

Example. Les tamales sont intéressants parce que c'est un aliment très populaire en Amérique latine. En plus, les tamales sont disponibles dans une grande variété de saveurs. Par exemple, les Mexicains préparent les tamales avec des feuilles de maïs, et en Amérique centrale, on utilise des feuilles de bananier. Et aussi, les gens remplissent les tamales avec différents types de viandes, fruits, épices et fromages.

... es interesante porque...

Además...

Por ejemplo...

También...

Example. Los tamales son interesantes porque son una comida muy popular en América Latina. Además, los tamales están disponibles en una variedad de sabores. Por ejemplo, en México, hacen tamales con hojas de maíz y en América Central los hacen con hojas de banano. También, las personas rellenan los tamales con diferentes carnes, frutas, especias y quesos.

....ist interessant, weil...

Zusätzlich...

Zum Beispiel...

Demnach...

Example: Tamales sind interessant, weil sie ein sehr populäres Gericht in Lateinamerika sind. Zusätzlich sind Tamales in einer Vielzahl von Geschmacksrichtungen erhältlich. Zum Beispiel werden Tamales in Mexiko mit Maisblättern und in Zentralamerika mit Bananenblättern zubereitet. Außerdem befüllen die Menschen Tamales mit verschiedenen Sorten Fleisch, Früchten, Gewürzen und Käsesorten.

4. Opinion

I like…….because….

….has…

….is…

People should try…

Example. I like cinnamon tea because it is delicious. The tea has great flavor. It is very refreshing on a cold morning. People should try cinnamon tea with their breakfast.

J'aime… parce que….

….a…

….est…

Il faut essayer…

Example. J'aime le thé à la cannelle parce que c'est délicieux. Le thé a un goût excellent. C'est très revigorant pour une froide matinée. il faut essayer le thé à la cannelle au petit déjeuner.

Me gusta… porque…

… tiene…

… es…

Las personas deberían probarlo. . .

Example. Me gusta el té de canela porque es delicioso. El té tiene un gran sabor. Es muy refrescante en una mañana fría. Las personas deberían probar el té de canela en su desayuno.

Ich mag…, weil…

….hat…

…ist…

Die Leute sollten …. probieren.

Example. Ich mag Zimt Tee, weil das köstlich ist. Der Tee hat einen guten Geschmack. Er ist sehr erfrischend an einem kalten Morgen. Die Leute sollten Zimttee beim Frühstück probieren.

Freewriting

Freewriting in a foreign language occurs when teachers provide a specific block of time in which students are given a chance to write on a topic. The topic selected should tap into students' background knowledge, either from their own personal experiences or from classroom discussions and reading.

Before writing on the topic, teachers practice the related vocabulary and sentence structures with the students. Students are then asked to write as much as they can, freely, on the topic. The focus of freewriting is to communicate meaning through copious amounts of writing in a timed period. Freewriting helps students develop fluency and confidence while experiencing a low-stress opportunity for output. Posted vocabulary, word walls, and sentences stems are appropriate during a freewriting activity; however, scaffolded paragraph frames would overstructure the writing and inhibit students' ability to develop fluency.

A NOTE ON CURRICULUM DESIGN

It is important to remember to use backward design when you are planning your lessons and when selecting your resources and activities. Start with the end in mind: the ACTFL Can-Do Statement you select to help your students reach a new level of language performance and to improve their proficiency. Once you have determined your benchmark and how you will assess it in the three modes of communication, you can select your authentic resource. Any of the structured conversations and reading and writing activities in this book can be used with many authentic resources. You need only scaffold the lessons in a way that makes them accessible to students. Using scaffolded exercises and structured activities can make authentic resources a valuable part of your curriculum. Integrated Performance Assessments (IPAs) are created using these techniques.

For the AP® Foreign Language Course Instructor and the IB Diploma Programme Language Acquisition Instructor

Students must be able to interpret information from an authentic text and use the information that they comprehend to engage in written interpersonal and presentational communication. They need to practice structured reading and writing activities to be able to successfully perform in the target language and show proficiency as necessary in their language assessments, including those on the AP® and IB exams.

The AP® achievement level descriptions for written communication at a level 5 require control and accuracy in language use and interpretation and an in-depth comprehension of text functions for both input and output of written language. These include "good control of culturally appropriate conventions" as well as an awareness of language structures, writing conventions, and register in their written interpersonal communication (College Board, n.d., p. 12- 13). They also require students' use of "paragraph-length discourse with mostly appropriate use of cohesive devices" (College Board, n.d., p. 22, 26).

The practice your students will engage in with Step 7 will provide exposure to good literacy practices in each mode of communication and will add to their ability to receive written language and engage in written communication. It is important that the opportunities you provide to your students reflect a variety of content and contexts so that they fully acquire the scope of literacy necessary for advanced proficiency. The more opportunities you give to your students to access language, the more experience they will have communicating in the target language.

Photo courtesy of Lamar CISD

Motivation

☐ Increasing opportunities for comprehension: The interactive nature of these structured activities lowers the affective filter for students, thus motivating them to remain engaged in the content.

☐ Fostering a sense of accomplishment: Students feel a sense of accomplishment when they are able to comprehend input and produce output in the target language. Structured activities provide such scaffolded opportunities for enhanced learning.

☐ Introducing culture in language learning: Selecting target language texts that provide opportunities to read and write about the cultures and countries that speak the target language can ignite students' interest in learning. Learning about target-language culture is inherently motivating to students and takes the focus off of grammar or "language" study momentarily.

Access to Language

☐ Providing increased exposure to language: Reading provides students with exposure to more words and structures in the target language than are available in any other source. This is even more powerful when students are engaged in Free Voluntary Reading and have freedom to choose a piece of text that they find engaging.

☐ Offering scaffolded sources of input: Cooperative reading and writing provide students with targeted exposure to specific language structures that can be customized to meet learners' levels of proficiency. For example, in the activity "T-Chart, Pair, Defend," teachers can provide specific stems that match students' varying proficiency levels so they can successfully partake in the exchange of information.

☐ Highlighting purpose that leads to understanding: The foundation of both structured reading and writing activities is to provide students with a purpose for reading and writing in the target language. When students are focused on why they are reading a specific piece of text and/or responding to a particular writing prompt, learning and comprehension are increased.

What additional research shows the effect of structured reading and writing activities on students' comprehension and language development?

Structured reading strategies are essential for creating deep comprehension of new learning. They also help to create effective processes that can be used to "cross-check" and make sense of new material. According to Marie Clay (1991), these strategies can become a process by which students search for meaning in their reading. In addition, reading strategies allow students the chance to engage in metacognition as they self-monitor their understanding of the text. Active instruction should include useful strategies that model what good readers do (Allington, 2002).

Extensive reading of self-selected texts creates stronger, more fluent, and more independent readers in the foreign language (Bamford & Day, 2004). This practice strengthens not only reading abilities but also listening, speaking, and writing.

Structured writing strategies are tools for learners. Fountas and Pinnell (2001) state that these strategies help students understand the structure of informational text. Working on a chart with students or having them work in pairs assures that students understand text at a deeper level.

"Task-focused students' talk and writing — collaborative use of language — is the medium through which students' knowledge of the world and knowledge about language emerges" (Gibbons, 2002, vii).

FAQ

German Alps

WHY DO MOST OF THE STRUCTURED READING ACTIVITIES REQUIRE STUDENTS TO WRITE?

To measure the effectiveness of structured reading activities, it is important to assess student comprehension. The thinking that occurs when students read is an internal process, and in order to assess student comprehension, we must create a path for making that process visible. Writing about the text provides a way for students to demonstrate their understanding of the reading. An alternative way to measure reading comprehension is to have students discuss what they have read. Students can discuss their reading in groups or with the teacher, using structured conversations or sentence stems. In essence, it isn't enough to ask students to read; they must read and make sense of the text. When students respond in writing or in conversation, it is easy to see what they have learned.

WHAT CAN I DO TO HELP MY STRUGGLING READERS AND WRITERS ACHIEVE SUCCESS DURING STRUCTURED READING AND WRITING ACTIVITIES?

We all have students who encounter difficulty in the classroom. To help those who struggle with reading and writing in a foreign language, teach with an "I do, we do, you do" mentality. This approach is a simplified way to foster student independence. Let's look at a structured writing activity called "Draw and Write" as an example. Our first step is to explicitly model the activity (I do). The teacher draws a picture of his or her thinking and then writes sentences that explain or support the drawing. Next, the teacher and the students draw a picture of their collective thinking and then interactively write sentences to clarify the picture (we do). Lastly, students draw and write independently (you do). More proficient students may only need one explicit example of this technique and one shared example in order to be successful independently, whereas our struggling students may need multiple modeled examples and many practice opportunities to master the activity.

Many teachers take class time to preview vocabulary and texts for the next day's lesson. This gives struggling students additional exposure to the material they will need. Three other ways to offer support are to provide an already completed example of the reading or writing task for students to reference; to use adapted texts with abbreviated language, and to maintain a dialogue journal with each student in order to identify and correct specific areas of confusion.

Step 7 ACTIVITIES

36. Embedded Reading *(Adapted from Seidlitz, Base, Lara, & Smith, 201(*

DESCRIPTION

Embedded Reading is a way of adapting text that enables students, especially those at lower levels of language proficiency, to receive comprehensible input while gaining access and comprehending grade-level text. In their respective works, Blaine Ray and Stephen Krashen encourage teachers to ensure that language learners have access to engaging reading texts. In order for students at the beginner/intermediate levels to read complex material, certain adjustments to texts are necessary.

DIRECTIONS

1. Choose a short text you want beginning or intermediate students to be able to read and comprehend.

2. Write a simpler version of the text line-by-line, simplifying clauses, removing adjectives and adverbs, and replacing lower-frequency vocabulary with higher-frequency vocabulary. This will become the intermediate-level text.

3. Rewrite the text again, further simplifying this new version. This is the beginner-level text. Make sure to eliminate complex clauses and to use repetitive grammatical structures as frequently as possible. Try to have no more than 7 words per sentence for this text. Give all students the simplest (beginner) text to read. They should scan the text for unfamiliar vocabulary, and you can provide the meanings of those words. Intermediate and more advanced students will breeze quickly through the beginning-level text.

4. Have all students read the intermediate text. Provide meanings for unfamiliar words they find through their scanning of the text (see pg. 113).

5. Repeat this process using the original text, making sure to provide meanings for unfamiliar words.

6. Expect the students to struggle with grammatical structures and meanings of words in the text. The goal is not to achieve complete comprehension of every aspect of the text, but to gain a general understanding of the text and to receive authentic comprehensible input.

Example:

ORIGINAL TEXT	INTERMEDIATE	BEGINNER
Although the vacation had included many unforeseen disasters, Eli was grateful for having had the opportunity to experience a new culture.	The vacation had many unforeseen problems. Eli was still grateful that he experienced a new culture.	There was a boy. The boy's name was Eli. Eli went on vacation. There were problems on the vacation. There were good things on the vacation, too. Eli was glad. He saw a new culture.

37. Interpretive Listening with Authentic Resources

DESCRIPTION

This activity is intended to practice listening for specific information. It can be adapted for any authentic resource where students can identify information that would respond to the five basic question words: *Who, What, When, Where, and Why*.

Qui?   Quoi?

Pourquoi?

Où?   Quand?

DIRECTIONS

1. Begin by identifying connections that the students may have to the function of the authentic resource listening activity. Brainstorm a list of language chunks and vocabulary on the board in the L1.

2. Inform students that they do not need to understand every word that is said in the listening activity, nor do they need perfect spelling in their graphic organizers and notes.

3. Review the question words in the target language. Write them on the board or on a large post-it note. Pass out the graphic organizers. Remind the students to write in simple phrases (language chunks) or words.

4. First listening and note taking: students will take notes in their graphic organizers. Share and brainstorm in groups after the first listening. Speak in the target language after the first listening. Assist students and groups that have difficulty by using physical gestures and simple words to reinforce the listening.

5. Review responses to the five questions as a whole class. Write responses on the board with the correct spelling. Remind students to notice the language in its written form and to make corrections to their graphic organizers. Additional teacher talk time can be added briefly to point out phonological and grammatical awareness in the target language.

6. Second listening and note taking: students will add additional information or depth of response to their graphic organizers. Add to the class responses during the listening if necessary. Call attention to the board, and allow the students time to notice any additions. Do not ask them to have an exact replica of what is written on the board.

7. Organize small-group interactions with follow-up questions and activities designed to reinforce individual learning. The completed graphic organizer can now be used as a resource.

Follow up questions must include *Who, What, When, Where, and Why*. They should reflect similar language use and function as the listening activity. These questions should be provided in writing but should not be written by the students. Students will practice responding to a level of language higher than their own. They will be speaking at a variety of levels, from simple words to language chunks to complete phrases. Do not grade this activity. Recordings may be used to review and reinforce language use in the future.

(Elizabeth Johnson)

Step 7 ACTIVITIES

38. Pass-Along-Papers

DESCRIPTION

This is an activity that I developed early on when I noticed how hesitant my students were to freewrite in the target language. I discovered that if they could see examples of how their classmates were responding to similar questions in writing, it may boost confidence for those more reticent to pick up their pens. Students simply respond to a series of questions in the target language, but they do so by passing papers back and forth (or in circle) to build on the writing of their peers. I've found students are much more motivated to write when they can see how their peers responded to the same questions.

DIRECTIONS

1. Structure the classroom configuration that day so students walk into a setup that is new to them. You can move student desks into small circles of four to six desks, or if that is your norm, you can adjust to rows of 4-6.

2. Depending on the number of "round tables" you can create (I could form six groups of five students per group), create a document with a series of five questions relating to unit vocabulary or text that is currently being discussed. The goal is that each student per group has a different question to answer.

3. Students number off one through five per group, and you start the timer. Students have two minutes to respond to the question that matches their number.

4. After time is up, students pass the paper to the person behind or to the right of them, depending on the seating arrangement.

5. Students then answer the same question that the classmate before them had answered, but they must answer in a different way, with different vocabulary, etc. This step provides modeling, so students can feel more confident in the correct way to respond.

6. Keep passing papers at two-minute intervals until each person has answered every question.

7. Randomly select documents to display on the document camera, and discuss the various responses. You can use these to point out grammar intricacies and remind students of rules.

For example:

1. What do you purchase at the grocery store?
   Stem: At the grocery store, I purchase…

2. Who goes to the grocery store in your family?
   Stem: In my family, _____ goes to the grocery store because….

   Possible responses: "My mother goes because she needs to cook dinner," "My father goes because he cooks breakfast for everyone," or "My grandmother goes because my mother is sick right now."

3. How will you pay for the items at the grocery store?
   Stem: At the grocery store, I will pay with the_____found in my_____

   Possible responses: backpack, wallet, purse, cash, credit card, Apple Pay, etc.

1. Qu'achetez-vous au supermarché?
   Amorce de phrase: Au supermarché, j'achète…

   Qui fait les courses chez vous?
   Amorce de phrase: Dans ma famille, c'est _____ qui fait les courses au supermarché, parce que…

   Réponses possibles: "Ma mère va au supermarché pour préparer le dîner," "Mon père y va parce qu'il prépare le petit déjeuner pour tout le monde," ou "C'est ma grand-mère qui va au supermarché parce que ma mère est malade en ce moment."

2. Comment allez-vous payer à la caisse du supermarché?
   Amorce de phrase: Au supermarché, je vais payer avec _____ que j'ai dans mon _____

   Réponses possibles: sac à dos, portefeuille, sac à main, argent liquide, carte de crédit, Apple Pay, etc.

Step 7 ACTIVITIES

1. ¿Qué compras en el supermercado?
   Fragmento: En el supermercado, compro...

2. ¿Quién va al supermercado en tu familia?
   Fragmento: En mi familia, _____ va al supermercado
   porque....

   Posibles respuestas: "Va mi madre porque necesita cocinar la
   cena," "Va mi padre porque prepara el desayuno para todos,"
   o "Va mi abuela porque mi madre ahora está enferma."

   ¿Cómo pagarás los artículos en el supermercado?
   Fragmento: En el supermercado, pagaré con_____ que
   encontré en mi_____

   Posibles respuestas: mochila, billetera, cartera, dinero en
   efectivo, tarjeta de crédito, Apple Pay, etc.

1. Was kauft man im Lebensmittelgeschäft?
   Stammsatz: Im Lebensmittelgeschäft kaufe ich...

2. Wer geht in deiner Familie Lebensmittel einkaufen?
   Stammsatz: In meiner Familie geht _____ Lebensmittel
   einkaufen, weil....

   Mögliche Antworten: "Meine Mutter geht, weil sie das Abendessen
   kochen muss," "Mein Vater geht, weil er Frühstück für alle zubereitet,"
   oder "Meine Großmutter geht, weil meine Mutter
   gerade krank ist."

   Wie bezahlst du für die Gegenstände im Lebensmittelgeschäft?
   Stammsatz: Im Lebensmittelgeschäft bezahle ich mit_____ aus
   meinem/r _____

   Mögliche Antworten: Rucksack, Geldbörse, Handtasche, Kreditkarte,
   Apple Pay, etc.

39. Read, Write, Pair, Share   *(Adapted from Kagan & Kagan, 2009)*

DESCRIPTION

This strategy encourages students to share their writing and ideas during interactions. Students read a text, write their thoughts using a sentence starter, pair with another student, and share their writing.

DIRECTIONS

1. Choose a text for the students to read.

2. Have students scan the text for unfamiliar vocabulary (see pg. 113).

3. Have students read the text individually.

4. Have students respond to a writing prompt about the text, either summarizing the text or sharing their points of view.

5. Randomly partner students, and have them share what they wrote.

Photo courtesy of Lamar CISD

EXTENSION → *After students share their writing, provide a second prompt, and repeat steps 4 and 5*

Step 7 ACTIVITIES

40. Letter Response

DESCRIPTION

This activity is very much like a chapter review or paragraph summary with a small twist. In Letter Response, students have a chance to inject their own curiosity and creativity while they use the target language in writing about real-world issues in the target culture and/or historical figures covered in the target-language curriculum.

DIRECTIONS

1. Review current topic vocabulary with students.

2. Have students write a letter to a classmate about an issue or topic related to vocabulary covered in the curriculum. For example, in a classroom that just learned the key vocabulary related to international travel, a student may write a letter about his or her experience printing a boarding pass, talking to a gate agent, and having his or her passport stamped at customs. Perhaps this student encountered a problem with this process or saw something interesting at the airport. This would be the topic of the letter.

3. Ask students to exchange letters with other students, and have them write a response to the letter they receive.

4. Have students give the letter and the response back to the original writer, and have the two students discuss each other's responses.

- Dear _____, I'm writing this letter to ask you about…

- I'm curious about why you decided to…

- How did you feel when…

- Dear _____, Thank you for your letter…

- I'd like to begin by explaining why…

- Cher / Chère _____, je vous écris pour vous demander...

- J'aimerais savoir pourquoi vous avez décidé de...

- Qu'avez-vous ressenti quand...

- Cher / Chère _____, je vous remercie pour votre lettre...

- Je voudrais d'abord expliquer les raisons pour lesquelles...

- Estimado _____: Escribo esta carta para consultarlo sobre…

- Me da curiosidad saber por qué decidió…

- ¿Cómo se sintió cuando…?

- Estimado _____: Gracias por su carta…

- Me gustaría empezar por explicar por qué…

- Liebe/r _____, ich schreibe diesen Brief, um dich/Sie nach ..... zu fragen.

- Ich würde gern erfahren, warum du/Sie entschieden hast/haben…

- Wie hast du dich/ haben Sie sich gefühlt, als…

- Liebe/r _____, danke für deinen/Ihren Brief…

- Ich würde gern beginnen, indem ich erkläre warum…

(Adapted from Seidlitz & Perryman, 2011)

Step 7 ACTIVITIES

41. Fortune Misfortune *(Adapted from Seidlitz & Perryman, 2011)*

DESCRIPTION

This activity places students in the midst of the unit or topic they are studying. They write from a first-person perspective about the unit or topic and are faced with making decisions that may have a positive or negative effect. Students gain deeper levels of understanding because they are personally invested in the topic.

Photo courtesy of Lamar CISD

Students take on the role of individuals who face advantages and disadvantages due to chance events and personal choices. This simulation enables students to experience the effects of personal decisions.

DIRECTIONS

1. Have students read about and discuss (in the target language) a historical or real-life situation that reflects the current topic of study or unit of vocabulary. Here are some examples: going on a trip to another country, a natural disaster, or going to a new school in a new country.

2. Brainstorm a list of possible fortunes and misfortunes that could happen in the chosen situation. The teacher writes these possibilities on index cards.

3. Have students write short paragraphs from the first-person perspective describing a day in their situations.

4. The teacher selects a fortune or misfortune card randomly from the deck.

5. Ask students to write a new paragraph describing how they responded to the fortune or misfortune. Continue to draw additional fortune/misfortune cards, and have students write new response paragraphs.

6. Have students share their writing with partners or as a whole class to conclude this assignment.

I am upset that... I am happy that... Sincerely, It is important... We need to... Nevertheless...	Cela m'énerve que... Je suis content que... Cordialement, C'est important... Nous devrions... Cependant...	Me molesta... Es excelente que... Sinceramente. Es importante... Debemos... No obstante...	Ich bin frustriert... Es ist wunderbar, dass... Beste Grüße Es ist wichtig... Wir müssen... Dennoch...

Brainstorm Sentence Stems
- I'd want to have…
- One thing we'd need is…
- _____ might be necessary to…

Typical Day Sentence Stems
- Today began with…
- First, I…
- I also had a chance to…

Fortune/Misfortune Sentence Stems
- It started when…
- Great news, today…
- Bad news, today…

Brainstorm Sentence Stems
- Je voudrais avoir…
- Nous aurions besoin de…
- _____ serait nécessaire pour…

Typical Day Sentence Stems
- Ma journée a commencé par…
- D'abord, je…
- J'ai aussi eu l'occasion de…

Fortune/Misfortune Sentence Stems
- Ça a commencé quand…
- Bonne nouvelle, aujourd'hui…
- Mauvaise nouvelle, aujourd'hui…

Brainstorm Sentence Stems
- Me gustaría tener…
- Una cosa que necesitamos es…
- _____ podría ser necesario…

Typical Day Sentence Stems
- Hoy comenzó con…
- Primero, yo…
- También tuve la oportunidad de…

Fortune/Misfortune Sentence Stems
- Comenzó cuando…
- Excelentes noticias, hoy…
- Malas noticias, hoy…

Brainstorm Sentence Stems
- Ich hätte gern…
- Eine Sache, die wir bräuchten ist…
- _____ könnte notwendig sein für…

Typical Day Sentence Stems
- Heute begann mit…
- Zuerst_____ich…
- Ich hatte auch die Möglichkeit…

Fortune/Misfortune Sentence Stems
- Es begann als…
- Großartige Neuigkeiten, heute…
- Schlechte Neuigkeiten, heute…

Step 7 ACTIVITIES

42. Writing Window *(Adapted from Seidlitz & Perryman, 2011)*

DESCRIPTION

In this activity, students are presented with an image that they are going to describe in detail. After students have a list of vocabulary to describe the image, they write a paragraph as if they were actually "inside" the image.

DIRECTIONS

1. Post an image that all students can clearly see.

2. Create class list of all vocabulary (in English and the target language) of any items seen in the image. For example:

• List everything you see in your image. • List adjectives that would describe the objects in the image. • Use verbs to identify the action you see in your image. • List what you would see, hear, and/or smell if you were actually in the image.	• Citez tout ce que vous voyez dans votre image. • Citez les adjectifs qui pourraient décrire les objets présents dans l'image. • Utilisez des verbes pour identifier l'action que vous voyez dans votre image. • Notez ce que vous pourriez voir, entendre et sentir si vous vous trouviez réellement dans l'image.
• Haz una lista de todo lo que ves en la imagen. • Haz una lista de todos los adjetivos que describirían los objetos en la imagen. • Usa verbos para identificar la acción que ves en la imagen. • Haz una lista de lo que verías, escucharías u olerías si realmente estuvieras en la imagen.	• Zähle alles auf, was du in deinem Bild siehst. • Zähle Adjektive auf, die die Objekte auf dem Bild beschreiben. • Benutze Verben, um auszudrücken welche Handlung du auf dem Bild siehst. • Zähle auf was du sehen, hören und/oder riechen würdest, wenn du tatsächlich in dem Bild wärst.

3. Tell the students to close their eyes, mentally step into the image, and look all around.

4. For more advanced students, the teacher can say,

"Now, what else do you see? List what you hear. List what you smell. List what the people are wearing and saying. Put your pencils down."

"Et que vois-tu d'autre? Que peux-tu entendre? Que peux-tu sentir? Comment les personnages sont-ils habillés et que disent-ils? Posez vos stylos."

"Ahora, ¿qué más ves? Haz una lista de lo que escuchas. Haz una lista de lo que hueles. Haz una lista de lo que están usando o diciendo las personas. Dejen sus lápices."

"Nun, was siehst du sonst noch? Zähle auf, was du hörst. Zähle auf, was du riechst. Zähle auf, was die Menschen tragen und sagen. Legt eure Stifte hin."

5. Have students write a paragraph as if they were present within the image.

6. After students complete their compositions, have them share their writing within the groups.

7. After sharing, students reveal the image that inspired their writing.

"Only a few months ago, we were dreaming about visiting France, and now I…"

"On Sunday afternoon we hired a chauffeur and drove out to see the palace of Versailles, and I…"

"There I stood on the Champs-Élysées, ready to take on all Paris had to offer, and I…"

"I slipped away from the tour group and rounded a corner near the old convent to witness the most glorious sight…"

"Il y a quelques mois seulement, nous rêvions de visiter la France, et maintenant je…"

"Le dimanche après-midi, nous avons pris un chauffeur pour aller visiter le château de Versailles, et je…"

"J'étais sur les Champs-Élysées, prêt à découvrir tout ce que Paris a à offrir, et je…"

"Je me suis éloigné du groupe et j'ai passé l'angle d'une rue près du vieux couvent pour profiter de la plus belle vue…"

"Hace solo unos meses atrás estábamos soñando con visitar Francia y ahora…"

"El domingo por la tarde contratamos un chofer y nos dirigimos a ver el Palacio de Versailles y…"

"Ahí estaba parado en el Campo Eliseos, listo para recibir todo lo que París tenía para ofrecerme y…"

"Me alejé del grupo de la excursión y doblé en la esquina cerca del viejo convento para poder ser testigo de la vista más gloriosa…"

"Vor ein paar Monaten haben wir davon geträumt Frankreich zu besuchen und nun…"

"Am Sonntagnachmittag haben wir einen Chauffeur angeheuert und sind zu dem Versailler Palast gefahren und ich…"

"Da stand ich nun auf der Champs-Élysées, bereit alles zu erleben, was Paris zu bieten hatte, und ich…"

"Ich entfernte mich von der Touristengruppe und ging um eine Ecke nahe dem alten Kloster und wurde Zeuge/in eines prachtvollen Anblick…"

Step 7 ACTIVITES

43. RAFT

DESCRIPTION

In the foreign language classroom, there are endless opportunities for writing dialogues and role-playing. This is a writing strategy that enables students to write from various points of view (Fisher & Frey, 2007). The letters stand for Role (the perspective the students take); Audience (the individuals the author is addressing); Format (the type of writing that will take place); Topic (the subject).

DIRECTIONS

Students write from various points of view, to various audiences, in different formats, and about different topics within the content.

1. Through assignment, choice, or a combination thereof, students are given a role, audience, format, and topic for their writing.

2. Depending on the purpose of the writing, the teacher might choose to standardize one or more of the components. For example, all students could be asked to write about the same topic, using the same format, and for the same audience. However, they could be assigned different roles. In another instance, students might be asked to write from the same role, on the same topic, and in the same format, but to different audiences.

The example below from Toni Theisen (2002) shows sample "roles" that students can choose from to demonstrate their understanding of a course unit, such as Traveling in France. Students have freedom to choose a role that appeals to them, and they are free to get creative in their writing. This activity opens the door to listening and speaking practice if students are paired for partner practice and then share their writing with classmates.

ROLE	AUDIENCE	FORMAT	TOPIC
Customer	Hotel employee	Letter	Make a reservation for several nights. Include all details.
Hotel employee	Customer	Reply letter	Confirm reservation details. Include changes.
Customer	Hotel Manager	Complaint	Demand compensation for problems and poor services.
Parisian real estate agency	Prospective renters	Real estate ad	Describe details of the aprments available for rent.
Students who want to study abroad	Study abroad organization	Application form for the program	Apply for rigorous study abroad program.
Students who stayed with a family	Family members	Thank you note	Thank the family for home stay and tell them about your return trip.

44. Language Experience Approach

DESCRIPTION

Language Experience Approach (LEA) is an approach to literacy that involves a teacher eliciting stories and experiences from a student or group of students (Nessel & Dixon, 2008). Examples of shared experiences could be class field trips, cultural/holiday programs in schools, lessons from a guest speaker, etc. As the stories and experiences are shared, the teacher transcribes the students' experiences. These transcriptions then become texts that the students use as literacy-building texts. Although the approach was developed in the context of native language literacy, it has also been used with some modifications in developing second language literacy.

DIRECTIONS

1. The five steps for conducting an LEA:

LANGUAGE SKILL	LEA STEP
Speaking and Listening	**STEP 1** Discuss a shared experience, such as a cultural or holiday program, field trip, lesson from a guest speaker, or classroom project.
Composing (Oral)	**STEP 2** As students discuss the experience in their own words (the best they can in the target language), the teacher reframes their statements, recording their thoughts on chart paper for all students to see. At this point, students are connecting oral to written language by seeing their own thoughts and words recorded on paper.
Listening and Reading	**STEP 3** Once the text is constructed, the teacher reads it out loud to the students, modeling the sounds of the target language with expression. Then with the teacher's help, students practice reading the text several times.
Developing Reading and Word Recognition	**STEP 4** The teacher guides the students in recognizing specific words and aids in their development of reading skills such as determining meaning from context, phonics, and structures of the language.
Writing	**STEP 5** Students then use the shared text as a springboard for writing original compositions.

(Adapted from Salva & Matis, 2017)

Step 7 ACTIVITIES

45. Reading Partners

DESCRIPTION

This activity "builds students' confidence and enjoyment of reading and discussion" (Bamford & Day, 2004, p. 49-50). Students are assigned a classmate with whom to plan and discuss reading.

DIRECTIONS

1. Pair off students based on student choice, teacher assignment, or scores on a reading placement test.

2. Explain that they will read as cooperative pairs, i.e., they will choose the same article or short story to read for homework.

3. Instruct each pair to browse through appropriate article and short story collections (in print or online) and choose which one they will both read. Each partner will have a copy of the chosen article or story.

4. Set aside time in class for pairs to discuss or share responses to what they have read. Partners will help each other with passages that are difficult to understand.

(Adapted from Bamford & Day, 2004)

46. Written Conversation *(Adapted from Seidlitz & Perryman, 2011)*

DESCRIPTION

This activity is a quick writing task designed to practice using vocabulary within the target language, using two different perspectives. Pairs of students can engage in a "Written Conversation" in the middle or the end of a unit of study.

DIRECTIONS

1. Have students brainstorm the attitudes and beliefs of two people in a given scenario related to the current unit of study.

2. Ask students to imagine something one character might say to the other if given the chance. Forms of communication may include texting, letter writing, or in-person conversation.

   Sentence Stems for Brainstorming:
   (Character) probably believes…
   (Character) might say…
   One word/phrase (Character) might say is…

3. Have students form partnerships as partner A and partner B to express points of view.

4. Have Partner A begin by writing a short note (text/letter/conversation script) to Partner B. Have Partner B read the note and write a short response on the same piece of paper and pass it back to Partner A. Have students continue this exchange for approximately ten minutes.

Dear _____, I'm writing to express my opinion about… You might want to consider the fact that… I must respectfully disagree with your thoughts about… I see we agree about…	Cher / Chère _____, je vous écris pour vous faire part de mon opinion au sujet de… Vous pourriez tenir compte du fait que… Je me permets d'exprimer mon désaccord avec votre opinion au sujet de… Je vois que nous sommes d'accord sur…
Estimado _____: Le escribo para expresar mi opinión sobre… Quizás quiera considerar el hecho de que… Disculpe, pero estoy en desacuerdo con su opinión sobre… Veo que estamos de acuerdo sobre…	Liebe/r_____ ich schreibe, um meine Meinung über… auszudrücken. Sie/du möchten/möchtest vielleicht über die Tatsache nachdenken, dass… Ich muss deinem/Ihrem Gedanken über… respektvoll widersprechen Ich sehe, wir sind uns einig über…

5. Have students discuss the notes as partners and then with the whole class.

An Overview of SLA Theories & Approaches

WHAT ARE THE DIFFERENT THEORIES AND APPROACHES TO LEARNING A SECOND LANGUAGE?

There are various theoretical ideas that exist about the best way to learn a new language. The following chart illustrates some of those theories, methods, or hypotheses throughout the years:

PRE 20TH CENTURY	EARLY 1900s	1940s, 1950s	1960s, 1970s	1980s, 1990s	1990s-PRESENT
Grammar Translation	Audiolingual, Direct Method	Behaviorist, S-R-R*	Universal Grammar/ Natural Approach, LAD**	Information Processing Models	Social Interaction and Sociocultural
	Bloomfield, Fries	Skinner	Chomsky, Krashen	Anderson, McLaughlin	Vygotsky

*Stimulus, Response and Reinforcement (S-R-R) **Language Acquisition Device (LAD)*

Grammar Translation

This method was based on teaching second language (L2) vocabulary, grammatical structures and whole texts, explained in the primary language (L1), but memorized and translated from L2 to L1 in order to read the classical literature of the new language. However, it was difficult to keep the learners interested and was not considered to be very effective for learning to communicate in a living spoken language.

Audiolingual Approach

This method focuses on the language learner acquiring grammatical structures through drill and practice. Instead of being directly taught grammar, students learn grammar through methods such as: repetition, inflection, replacement, and restatement.

Behaviorist Theory

This method predicted that behavior could be learned and performed through stimulus, response, and reinforcement. It involved a lot of repetition of grammatical forms in the second language. Positive feedback was given if the response was correct and negative feedback if the response was incorrect. The use of the first language was avoided as much as possible.

Universal Grammar Theory

Noam Chomsky is credited with creating the idea that human beings are born with the ability to learn any language. This theory argues that there are properties that all languages share (e.g., verbs, nouns, modifiers) and that humans from birth acquire all the elements of their first language (L1), including the grammar "rules," through observing and experimenting. The goal of instruction is to help the language learner adjust her/his first language knowledge according to the rules of the new language. Example: Spanish-speakers use the preposition "en" to indicate the location of objects on the surface of things ("on") as well as inside of another object ("in").

The Natural Approach

Stephen Krashen developed this method in the 1970s using ideas from Chomsky. His theory follows five hypotheses:

1. There is a natural order for learning a second language. Generally, the stages of language development include babbling and echolalic babbling (infancy), unitary stage (approx. age 2), expansion stage (approx. age 4), structural awareness stage (approx. age 5), automatic stage (approx. kindergarten), creative stage (approx. grade 1), and communication development (approx. grades 2-6). In Texas, teachers studying for certification do not need to memorize these labels, but they should understand the general flow of language development.

2. There is a difference between language acquisition and language learning. Teachers of language learners should strive to promote classroom experiences that aid in the acquisition of language. The more authentic the experience, the more likely it is to be internalized and remembered. Acquisition is a subconscious process in which the affective filter is low.

   It is dependent upon the teacher providing comprehensible and compelling input. The focus is on function over form.

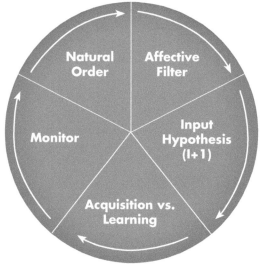

3. In language acquisition, the learner acquires the language in a natural way. When the learner learns a language consciously, the learner monitors and corrects what he/she is able to correct. Think of it as a type of mental inspection that is performed on the words or phrases that are about to be spoken. Students want to produce correct syntax/grammar, but their use of the monitor is limited only to those rules they know. When second language learners feel compelled to use the monitor in language production, fluency is hampered. As a rule, teachers can help second language learners become aware of what kinds of interactions are not dependent upon "correct usage" and which ones are.

4. The cause of second language learning is comprehensible input. In other words, if the input is comprehensible, the learner will understand and learn the language.

To read more about comprehensible input and how to deliver instruction that is comprehensible for second language learners, refer to pgs. 25 and 32.

5. The Affective Filter, that is emotions/feelings (relaxed vs. anxious and fearful), causes the student to learn or not learn the new language. Teachers have significant impact on whether or not a language learner's affective filter is "high" or "low." Some ways in which a teacher can lower the affective filter include: asking the language learner to perform at their level of proficiency after they demonstrate their readiness to do so, creating a friendly learning environment, increasing processing time/wait time, avoiding correcting errors in production (especially in front of peers), and allowing students opportunities to rehearse their responses.

Information Processing Approach

This approach considers that the ability to learn language is determined by a highly complex cognitive structure and that human knowledge is divided into declarative (storing information in long-term memory) and procedural knowledge (learning how to do something successfully).

Social Interaction and Sociocultural Theories

These theories indicate that everything is learned socially and that the role of language in the learner's environment through conversational interactions builds the knowledge on the second language.

Activities Index

Bibliography

ACTFL. (2010, May 22). Retrieved from: https://www.actfl.org/news/position-statements/use-the-target-language-the-classroom

Adams, M. J. (1994). *Beginning to read: Thinking and learning about print.* Cambridge, MA: MIT Press.

Allington, R. L. (2002). What I've learned about effective reading instruction: From a decade of studying exemplary elementary classroom teachers. *Phi Delta Kappan, 83*(10), 740-747.

Asher, J. (1969). The total physical response approach to second language learning. *The Modern Language Journal, 53*(1), 3-17.

Bamford, J., & Day, R. (2004). *Extensive reading activities for language teaching.* Cambridge, UK: Cambridge University Press.

Bickel, W. E., & Bickel, D. D. (1986). Effective schools, classrooms, and instruction: Implications for special education. *Exceptional Children, 52*(6), 489-500.

Callahan, R.M., Wilkinson, L., Muller, C., & Frisco, M. (2008). ESL placement and schools: Effects on immigrant achievement. *Educational Policy, 23*(2), 355-384.

Chamot, A. U. (2004). Issues in language learning strategy research and teaching. *Electronic Journal of Foreign Language Teaching, 1*(1), 14-26. Retrieved from: http://e-flt.nus.edu.sg/v1n12004/chamot.pdf

Clay, M. M. (1991). *Becoming literate: The construction of inner control.* Portsmouth, NH: Heinemann Educational Books.

College Board. AP French Language and Culture Course and Exam Description. Retrieved from: http://media.collegeboard.com/digitalServices/pdf/ap/ap-french-course-and-exam-description.pdf

Cook, V. (2008). *Second language learning and language teaching.* London, UK: Routledge.

Csíkszentmihályi, M. (2009). *Flow: the psychology of optimal experience.* New York, NY: Harper Row.

Dörnyei, Z., & Csizér, K. (1998). Ten commandments for motivating language learners: Results of an empirical study. *Language Teaching Research, 2*(3), 203-229.

Duffy, G. G. (2002). The case for direct explanation of strategies. In C.C. Block & M. Pressley (Eds.), *Comprehension instruction: Research-based best practices* (pp. 28-41). New York, NY: Guilford.

Echevarria, J., & Graves, A. W. (2015). *Sheltered content instruction: Teaching English language learners with diverse abilities.* Boston, MA: Pearson.

Echevarria, J., Vogt, M.E., & Short, D. (2017). *Making content comprehensible for English learners: The SIOP Model (5th edition).* New York, NY: Pearson.

Escalante, L.B. (2018). *Motivating ELLs.* Irving, TX: Seidlitz Education. Manuscript submitted for publication.

Fisher, D., & Frey, N. (2007). *Checking for understanding: Formative assessment techniques for your classroom.* Alexandria, VA: Association for Supervision and Curriculum Development.

Fountas, I. C., & Pinnell, G. S. (2001). *Guiding readers and writers, grades 3-6: Teaching comprehension, genre, and content literacy.* Portsmouth, NH: Heinemann.

Gardner, R. C., & Lambert, W. E. (1972). *Attitudes and motivation in second-language learning.* Rowley, MA: Newbury House Publishers.

Gardner, R. C., & Tremblay, P.F. (1994). On motivation, research agendas, and theoretical frameworks. *Modern Language Journal, 78,* 359-368.

Gardner, R. C. (2010). *Motivation and second language acquisition: The socio-educational model.* New York, NY: Peter Lang Publishing.

Gass, S. M., & Selinker, L. (2008). *Second language acquisition: An introductory course.* New York, NY: Routledge.

Geva, E. (2006). Second-language oral proficiency and second-language literacy. In D. August & T. Shanahan (Eds.), *Developing literacy in second-language learners: Report of the National Literacy Panel on Language-Minority Children and Youth,* (pp. 123-139). Mahwah, NJ: Lawrence Erlbaum.

Gewertz, C. (2005). Training focuses on teachers' expectations. *Education Week, 24*(30), 1-14.

Gibbons, P. (2002). *Scaffolding language, scaffolding learning: Teaching second language learners in the mainstream classroom.* Portsmouth, NH: Heinemann.

Gibbons, P. (2015). *Scaffolding language, scaffolding learning: Teaching second language learners in the mainstream classroom (2nd edition).* Portsmouth, NH: Heinemann.

Grabe, W. (2004). Research on teaching reading. *Annual Review of Applied Linguistics, 24,* 44 –69.

Grabe, W. (2009). *Reading in a second language: Moving from theory to practice.* Cambridge Applied Linguistics.

Grosjean, F. (2010). Who is bilingual? *Psychology Today.* Retrieved on January 23, 2018 from: https://www.psychologytoday.com/blog/life-bilingual/201010/who-is-bilingual

Hadley, A. O. (2001). *Teaching language in context* (3rd ed.). Boston, MA: Heinle and Heinle.

Hall, J. K. (2010). Interaction as method and result of language learning. *Language Teaching, 43*(2), 202-215.

Holden, B., & Usuki, M. (1999). Learner autonomy in language learning: A preliminary investigation. *Bulletin of Hokuriku University, 23,* 191-203.

Horwitz, E. K. (1986). Preliminary evidence for the reliability and validity of a foreign language anxiety scale. *TESOL Quarterly, 20*(3), 559-562.

Horwitz, E. K. (1996). Even teachers get the blues: Recognizing and alleviating language teachers' feelings of foreign language anxiety. *Foreign Language Annals, 29,* 365-372.

Horwitz, E. K., Horwitz, M., & Cope, J. A. (1986). Foreign language classroom anxiety. *Modern Language Journal, 70,* 125

Horwitz, E. K. (2013). *Becoming a language teacher: A practical guide to second language learning and teaching* (2nd edition). Boston, MA: Pearson Education, Inc.

IB Organization: International education. (n.d.). Retrieved from: http://www.ibo.org/ and http://www.ibo.org/globalassets/publications/recognition/2_langbsl.pdf

Jenkins, J. R., Stein, M. L., & Wysocki, K. (1984). Learning vocabulary through reading. *American Educational Research Journal, 21*(4), 767-787.

Jensen, E. (2005). *Teaching with the brain in mind.* Alexandria, VA: ASCD.

Johnson, D. W., & Johnson, R. T. (1999). Making cooperative learning work. *Theory into Practice, 38*(2), 67-73.

Johnson, T. C., Stoner, G., & Green, S. K. (1996). Demonstrating the experimenting society model with classwide behavior management interventions. *School Psychology Review, 25*(2), 199-214.

Kagan, S. & Kagan, M. (2009). *Kagan cooperative learning.* San Clemente, CA: Kagan Publishing.

Knapp, F.A. & Desrochers, M.N. (2009). An experimental evaluation of the instructional effectiveness of a student response system: Comparison with constructed overt responding. *International Journal of Teaching and Learning in Higher Education, 21*(1), 36-46.

Krashen, S. (1981). *Second language acquisition and second language learning.* New York, NY: Prentice-Hall.

Krashen, S. (1982). *Principles and practice in second language acquisition.* Oxford, UK: Pergamon.

Krashen, S. (2011). *Free voluntary reading.* Santa Barbara, CA: Libraries Unlimited, ABC-CLIO, LLC.

Lee, J. F., & VanPatten, B. (2003). *Making communicative language teaching happen.* Boston, MA: McGraw-Hill.

Leeman, J. (2003). Recasts and second language development. *Studies in Second Language Acquisition, 25*(01), 37-63.

Lemov, D. (2010). *Teach like a champion: 49 techniques that put students on the path to college (K-12).* San Francisco, CA: Jossey-Bass.

Lewis, M. (1993). The lexical approach (Vol. 1). Hove, UK: Language Teaching Publications.

Lipson, M., & Wixson, K. (2008). A*ssessment and instruction of reading and writing difficulties: An interactive approach* (3rd edition). New York, NY: Longman.

Long, M. H. (1981). Input, interaction, and second-language acquisition. *Annals of the New York Academy of Sciences, 379,* 259-278.

Long, M. H. (1996). The role of the linguistic environment in second language acquisition. In W. Ritchie, & T. Bhatia (Eds.), *Handbook of Language Acquisition: Vol. 2. Second Language Acquisition* (pp. 413–468). San Diego, CA: Academic Press.

Long, M. H. (2007). Recasts in SLA: The story so far. In Long, M. H. (Ed.), *Problems in SLA,* (pp. 75-116). Mahweh, NJ: Erlbaum.

Lyman, F. (1981). The responsive classroom discussion: The inclusion of all students. In A. Anderson (Ed.), *Mainstreaming Digest,* (pp. 109-113). College Park, MD: University of Maryland Press

Marzano, R. J., Pickering, D., & Pollock, J. E. (2001). *Classroom instruction that works: Research-based strategies for increasing student achievement.* Alexandria, VA: ASCD.

Marzano, R. J. (2004). *Building background knowledge for academic achievement: Research on what works in schools.* Alexandria, VA: ASCD.

Matis, A.F. (2013). T*he art of saving a language: heritage language learning in America* (Master's thesis). The University of Texas at Austin. Retrieved from: https://repositories.lib.utexas.edu/handle/2152/24063

McDougall, D., & Cordeiro, P. (1992). Effects of random questioning expectations on education majors' preparedness for lecture and discussion. *College Student Journal, 26*(2), 193-198.

McLaughlin, M. (2003). *Guided comprehension in the primary grades.* Newark, DE: International Reading Association.

Meece, J. L., & Holt, K. (1993). A pattern analysis of students' achievement goals. *Journal of Educational Psychology, 85*(4), 582.

Motley, N. (2016). *Talk, read, talk, write: A practical routine for learning in all content areas (K-12).* Irving, TX: Seidlitz Education.

Moudraia, O. (2001). Lexical approach to second language teaching. Washington, DC: Center for Applied Linguistics. (ERIC Digest, EDO-FL-01-02). Retrieved from: http://www.cal.org/resources/digest/0102lexical.html

National Institute of Child Health and Human Development. (2000). *Teaching children to read: An evidence-based assessment of the scientific research literature on reading and its implications for reading instruction: Reports of the sub-groups.* (Report of the National Reading Panel, NIH, 00-4754. Washington, DC: US Government Printing Office.

Nessel, D., & Dixon, C. (Eds.). (2008). *Using the language experience approach with English language learners: Strategies for engaging students and developing literacy.* Thousand Oaks, CA: Corwin Press.

Norris, J. M., & Ortega, L. (2000). Effectiveness of L2 instruction: A research synthesis and quantitative meta-analysis. *Language Learning, 50*(3), 417-528.

Ortega, L. (2009). *Understanding second language acquisition.* New York, NY: Hodder Education.

Pulido, D. (2009). Developing reading skills in a foreign/second language. In A. Cirocki (Ed.), *Extensive Reading in English Language Teaching,* (pp. 27- 45). Munich, Germany: LINCOM EUROPA Studies in Second Language Teaching.

Ray, B., & Seely, C. (2015). *Fluency through TPR storytelling: Achieving real language acquisition in school.* Eagle Mountain, UT: Blaine Ray Workshops.

Salva, C., & Matis, A. (2017). *Boosting achievement: Reaching students with interrupted or minimal education.* Irving, TX: Seidlitz Education.

Santa, C. M., Havens, L. T. & Valdes, B. (2004). *Project CRISS (3rd edition),* Dubuque, IA: Kendell-Hunt.

Sardegna, V. (2012). Class notes from Methods of Teaching a Second/Foreign Language. Austin, TX: The University of Texas at Austin.

Sardegna, V. G., Lee, J. H., & Kusey, C. (2014). Development and validation of the learner attitudes and motivations for pronunciation (LAMP) inventory. System, 47, 162–175. https://doi.org/10.1016/J.SYSTEM.2014.10.009

Schmidt, R. W. (2001). Attention. In P. Robinson (Ed.), *Cognition and second language instruction,* (pp. 3-32). New York, NY: Cambridge University Press.

Schmoker, M. (2006). *Results now.* Alexandria, VA: Association for Supervision and Curriculum Development.

Seidlitz, John. (2011). *38 Great academic language builders: Activities for math, science, social studies, language arts...and just about everything else.* Irving, TX: Seidlitz Education.

Seidlitz, J., Base, M., & Lara, M. (2014). *ELLs in Texas: What administrators need to know.* Irving, TX: Seidlitz Education.

Seidlitz, J., Base, M., Lara, M., & Smith, H. (2016). *ELLs in Texas: What teachers need to know.* Irving, TX: Seidlitz Education.

Seidlitz, J., & Castillo, M. (2013). *Language and literacy for ELLs: Creating a systematic change for academic language.* Irving, TX: Seidlitz Education.

Seidlitz, J., & Castillo, M. (2010). *Language and literacy for ELLs workbook.* Irving, TX: Seidlitz Education.

Seidlitz, J., & Kenfield, K. (2011). *38 great academic language builders: Activities for math, science, social studies, language arts...and just about everything else.* Irving, TX: Seidlitz Education.

Seidlitz, J. & Perryman, B., (2011). *7 steps to a language-rich, interactive classroom: Research-based strategies for engaging all students.* Irving, TX: Seidlitz Education.

Snow, C. E., Griffin, P. & Burns, M. S. (2005). *Knowledge to support the teaching of reading: Preparing teachers for a changing world.* San Francisco, CA: Jossey-Bass.

Stahl, S. A., & Fairbanks, M. M. (1986). The effects of vocabulary instruction: A model-based meta-analysis. *Review of Educational Research, 56*(1), 72-110.

Swain, M. (1985). Communicative competence: Some roles of comprehensible input and comprehensible output in its development. Input in *Second Language Acquisition, 15,* 165-179.

Swain, M. (1995). Three functions of output in second language learning. In G. Cook, & B. Seidlhofer (Eds.), *Principle and practice in applied linguistics: Studies in honour of H. G. Widdowson,* (pp. 125-144). Oxford, UK: Oxford University Press.

Theisen, T. (2002). Differentiated instruction in the foreign language classroom: Meeting the diverse needs of all learners. *Communique: Languages other than English (LOTE) CED,* (6). Retrieved from: https://www.sedl.org/loteced/communique/n06.pdf

VanPatten, B., & Williams, J. (Eds.). (2014). *Theories in second language acquisition: An introduction.* New York, NY: Routledge.

VanPatten, B. (2014). Creating comprehensible input and output - fundamental considerations in language learning. *The Language Educator, 9*(5), 24-26. Retrieved December 15, 2017 from: https://www.actfl.org/sites/default/files/images/TLE/TLE_OctNov14_Article.pdf.

Vogt, M., & Nagano, P. (2003). Turn it on with light bulb reading! Sound-switching strategies for struggling readers. *The Reading Teacher, 57*(3), 214-221.

Vygotsky, L. S. (1986). *Thought and language, (Revised edition).* A. Kozulin, (Ed.). Cambridge, MA: MIT Press.

Webb, S. (2008). The effects of context on incidental vocabulary learning. *Reading in a Foreign Language, 20*(2), 232.

Wilson, C. D. (2016, April 29). How to give students more control over their learning. Retrieved December 15, 2017 from: https://www.edweek.org/tm/articles/2016/03/08/give-students-more-control-over-their-learning.html

Yzquierdo, M. (2017). *Pathways to greatness for ELL newcomers: A comprehensive guide for schools and teachers.* Irving, TX: Seidlitz Education.

Anna Matis

is a writer and consultant for Seidlitz Education. Her love of language learning stems from childhood experiences as an immigrant and ESL student from Budapest, Hungary. Proficient in multiple languages, she is passionate about second language acquisition for all ages, sheltered instruction strategies, heritage language learning, and long-term ELL research. She is a former high school French teacher and has led professional development at the state and national level, coached teachers in language learning strategies, and created instructional products for both teachers and administrators working with ESL students. Anna recently coauthored *Boosting Achievement: Reaching Students with Interrupted or Minimal Education.*

John Seidlitz

is an independent educational consultant and the author of *Sheltered Instruction in Texas: A Guide for Teachers of ELLs; Navigating the ELPS: Using the New Standards to Improve Instruction for English Learners;* and *7 Steps to a Language-Rich, Interactive Classroom®.* Mr. Seidlitz has been a member of the SIOP® National faculty and guest lecturer for many regional and national language development conferences. He taught social studies and ESL, served as a secondary ESL program coordinator, and held the position of education specialist at ESC Region 20 in San Antonio, Texas. In 2005, Mr. Seidlitz founded Seidlitz Education, which is dedicated to the mission of Giving Kids the Gift of Academic Language™.

SEIDLITZ EDUCATION BOOK ORDER FORM

   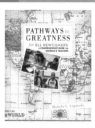  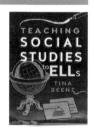

TITLE	PRICE	QTY	TOTAL$
38 Great Academic Language Builders	$24.95		
7 Pasos para crear un aula interactiva y rica en lenguaje SPANISH	$29.95		
7 Steps to a Language-Rich Interactive Classroom	$29.95		
7 Steps To a Language-Rich, Interactive Foreign Language Classroom	$32.95		
Boosting Achievement: Reaching Students with Interrupted or Minimal Education	$26.95		
Content Review & Practice for the TX ESL 154	$39.95		
Content Review & Practice for the TX Bilingual 164	$39.95		
Content Review & Practice for the TX Spanish 190	$39.95		
Diverse Learner Flip Book	$26.95		
ELLs in Texas: What Teachers Need to Know 2ND ED.	$34.95		
ELs in Texas: What School Leaders Need to Know 3RD ED.	$34.95		
ELPS Flip Book	$19.95		
English/Spanish Linguistic and Academic Connections	$29.95		
Mi Cuaderno de Dictado SPANISH	$7.95		
Motivating ELLs: 27 Activities to Inspire & Engage Students	$26.95		
COLUMN 1 TOTAL $			

TITLE	PRICE	QTY	TOTAL$
Navigating the ELPS: Using the Standards to Improve Instruction for English Learners	$24.95		
Navigating the ELPS: Math 2ND EDITION	$29.95		
Navigating the ELPS: Science	$29.95		
Navigating the ELPS: Social Studies	$29.95		
Navigating the ELPS: Language Arts and Reading	$34.95		
Optimizando el desarrollo de la lectoescritura SPANISH	$39.95		
Pathways to Greatness for ELL Newcomers: A Comprehensive Guide for Schools & Teachers	$32.95		
Reading & Writing with English Learners	$29.95		
RTI for ELLs Fold-Out	$16.95		
Sheltered Instruction in Texas: Second Language Acquisition Methods for Teachers of ELs	$29.95		
Talk Read Talk Write: A Practical Routine for Learning in All Content Areas K-12 2ND ED.	$32.95		
Teaching Social Studies to ELLs	$24.95		
Teaching Science to English Learners	$24.95		
¡Toma la Palabra! SPANISH	$32.95		
Vocabulary Now! 44 Strategies All Teachers Can Use	$29.95		
COLUMN 2 TOTAL $			

Pricing, specifications, and availability subject to change without notice.

COLUMN 1+2	$
DISCOUNT	$
SHIPPING	$
TAX	$
TOTAL	$

SHIPPING 9% of order total, minimum $14.95
5-7 business days to ship. If needed sooner please call for rates.
TAX EXEMPT? please fax a copy of your certificate along with order.

HOW TO ORDER

PHONE **(210) 315-7119** | ONLINE at **www.seidlitzeducation.com**

FAX completed form with payment info to **(949) 200-4384**

NAME _____

SHIPPING ADDRESS _____   CITY _____   STATE, ZIP _____

PHONE NUMBER _____   EMAIL ADDRESS _____

TO ORDER BY FAX
to **(949) 200-4384**
please complete
credit card info *or*
attach purchase order

☐ Visa ☐ MasterCard ☐ Discover ☐ AMEX

CARD # _____   EXPIRES _____
mm/yyyy

SIGNATURE _____   CVV _____
3- or 4- digit code

☐ **Purchase Order attached**
please make
P.O. out to
Seidlitz Education

For information about Seidlitz Education products
and professional development, please contact us at

(210) 315-7119 | kathy@johnseidlitz.com
56 Via Regalo, San Clemente, CA 92673
www.seidlitzeducation.com

Giving kids the
gift of **academic
language.**™

REV050321

Three ways to order

{
- **FAX** completed order form with payment information to **(949) 200-4384**
- **PHONE** order information to **(210) 315-7119**
- **ORDER ONLINE** at **www.seidlitzeducation.com**

Pricing, specifications, and availability subject to change without notice.

TITLE	Price	QTY	TOTAL $
Instead Of I Don't Know Poster, 24" x 36"			
☐ Elementary ENGLISH	$9.95		
☐ Secondary ENGLISH	$9.95		
20 pack **Instead Of I Don't Know** Posters, 11" x 17"			
☐ Elementary ENGLISH	$40.00		
☐ Secondary ENGLISH	$40.00		
Instead Of I Don't Know Poster, 24" x 36" Elementary SPANISH	$9.95		
20 pack **Instead Of I Don't Know** Posters, 11" x 17" Elementary SPANISH	$40.00		
		TOTAL $	

TITLE	Price	QTY	TOTAL $
NEW! **Instead Of I Don't Know** Poster For the LOTE Classrom 24" x 36"			
☐ LOTE FRENCH	$9.95		
☐ LOTE SPANISH	$9.95		
☐ LOTE GERMAN	$9.95		
☐ LOTE ARABIC	$9.95		
☐ LOTE CHINESE	$9.95		
		TOTAL $	

	TITLE	Price	QTY	TOTAL $
Please speak in complete sentences.	**Please Speak In Complete Sentences** Poster 24" x 36" ☐ ENGLISH ☐ SPANISH	$9.95		
	20 pack **Please Speak In Complete Sentences** Posters, 11" x 17" ☐ ENGLISH ☐ SPANISH	$40.00		
			TOTAL $	

TITLE	Price	QTY	TOTAL $
Academic Language Cards and Activity Booklet, ENGLISH	$19.95		
Academic Language Cards, SPANISH	$9.95		
		TOTAL $	

SHIPPING 9% of order total, minimum $14.95
5-7 business days to ship.
If needed sooner please call for rates.

TAX EXEMPT? please fax a copy of your certificate along with order.

GRAND TOTAL	$
DISCOUNT	$
SHIPPING	$
TAX	$
FINAL TOTAL	$

NAME _____

SHIPPING ADDRESS _____   CITY _____   STATE, ZIP _____

PHONE NUMBER _____   EMAIL ADDRESS _____

TO ORDER BY FAX
to **(949) 200-4384**
please complete
credit card info *or*
attach purchase order

☐ Visa ☐ MasterCard ☐ Discover ☐ AMEX

CARD # _____   EXPIRES _____ mm/yyyy

SIGNATURE _____   CVV _____

☐ **Purchase Order**

please make
P.O. out to
Seidlitz Education